Communication and Human Rights

Aliaa Dakroury

Foreword by
Cees J. Hamelink

Kendall Hunt
publishing company

Cover image (hands) copyright © JupiterImages, Corp.
Image (abstract grey) copyright © Elen, 2009, under license from Shutterstock

Kendall Hunt
publishing company

www.kendallhunt.com
Send all inquiries to:
4050 Westmark Drive
Dubuque, IA 52004-1840

Copyright © 2009 by Kendall Hunt Publishing Company

ISBN 978-0-7575-6406-2

All rights reserved. No part of this publication may be reproduced, stored in a retrieval system, or transmitted, in any form or by any means, electronic, mechanical, photocopying, recording, or otherwise, without the prior written permission of the copyright owner.

Printed in the United States of America
10 9 8 7 6 5 4 3 2 1

With Love to the Inspiring People in My Life

My Wonderful Parents: *Anouna* and *Gedou* …

My Beloved Husband: *Mahmoud* …

My Lovely Children: *Yomna, Ahmed,* and *Yassmeen* …

Contents

About the Author vii

Foreword—*Cees J. Hamelink* ix

CHAPTER 1

Introduction: Is Communication a Basic Human Right? 1

CHAPTER 2

Early Context of the Right to Communicate 13

    American Bill of Rights 15
    The French Revolution and *La Déclaration des Droits
    de l'Homme et du Citoyen* 17
    Languaging the *Universal Declaration
    of Human Rights* 26
    Article (19) 29
    Beyond the *Universal Declaration of Human Rights* 31
    UNESCO Media Declaration 34
    The Flow of Information Debate 37
    The MacBride Commission 41

CHAPTER 3

A Debate on What Is a Right to Communicate 51

    Totalitarianism and Propaganda 52
    Hate Speech versus Free Speech 55
    The Internet, Pornography, and Offensive Signs 57
    Invasion of Privacy and the Right
    "Not to Communicate" 59
    Media Ownership and Control 63
    A Provisional Conceptualization of What Is a "Right" 65

CHAPTER 4

Philosophical Foundation of Communication as a "Human Right" 83

    John Milton (1608–1674): Early Uni-Dimensional Right ... 84
    John Locke (1632–1704): Absolute Individual Freedom ... 91
    Baron de Montesquieu (1689–1755): Legal Realization of Liberties 96
    Voltaire (1694–1778): Absolute Freedom of Speech 99
    Jeremy Bentham (1748–1832): Public Opinion and Freedom of Expression 104
    John Stuart Mill (1806–1873): Absolute Right Relative to Greatest Happiness 108

CHAPTER 5

Toward a Theorization of Communication as a "Human Right" 117

    John Dewey (1864–1952): Communication as a Social Dialogue 118
    Jürgen Habermas (1929–): Undistorted Communication 124
    Herbert Schiller (1919–2000): A Right to Communicate Cultures 136

CHAPTER 6

The Question of the Right to Communicate 159

    The Language Answer 159
    The Realization Phase 160
    The Practice Debate 162
    Perspectives on the Right to Communicate 166
    Is Communication a Basic Human Right? 170

References 175
Author Index 189
Subject Index 195

About the Author

Aliaa Dakroury, Ph.D., is a Lecturer at the Departments of Communication, Sociology, and Law at Carleton University, Ottawa, Canada. Her work concentrates on the examination of communication and human rights. Her areas of interest include: the Right to Communicate, media policy, history of ideas, international communication, Diaspora, globalization, ICTs, women rights, media representations, and Islam.

Dr. Dakroury is editor of *The Right to Communicate: Historical Hopes, Global Debates, and Future Premises* (with M. Eid and Y. R. Kamalipour, 2009), editor of the Fall 2008 special issue on the "Right to Communicate" in the *Global Media Journal—American Edition*, and co-editor of *Introduction to Communication and Media Studies* (with M. Eid, 2008). She is the author of numerous peer-reviewed journal articles and book chapters. Her work appears in *The Canadian Journal of Communication*; *Journal of Intergroup Relations*; *Culture, Language, and Representation Journal*; *Reconstruction: Studies in Contemporary Culture Journal*; *Media Development*; *American Journal of Islamic Social Sciences*; and *The Journal of International Communication*.

Dr. Dakroury is the winner of the Canadian Communication Association's 2005 *Van Horne Award*. She is a member of many human rights organizations, including the Right to Communicate Group, International Freedom of Expression eXchange (IFEX), World Association for Christian Communication (WACC), among many others. She serves on the editorial board of the *Global Media Journal—American Edition*. She was recently nominated as honorary expert in the Islamic Resource Bank (IRB): A joint project of the Minaret of Freedom Institute, the American Association of Muslim Social Scientists and the International Institute of Islamic Thought.

She received her Ph.D. and M.A. in Communication from Carleton University's School of Journalism and Communication, Ottawa, Canada, and B.A. from Cairo University's Faculty of Mass Media, Egypt. She can be reached at: *adakrour@connect.carleton.ca*.

Foreword

Cees J. Hamelink

There is an impressive library of books written about human communication. There are also rich volumes of studies produced on the subject of human rights. There is a remarkable paucity of scholarly works that combine these two domains: communication and human rights. If the combination occurs it is usually in the limited sense of addressing such issues as the protection of privacy or concerns about freedom of speech. Therefore, it was about time someone offered a broad study in which communication was conceptualized as a fundamental human entitlement and in which the historical context of that conceptualization was diligently reported and analyzed.

Aliaa Dakroury has now repaired this theoretical omission and there is good reason to be thankful for her pertinent contribution to a complicated global debate that will be a subject of debate and analysis for a considerable time to come. So far, this debate has been very controversial and contested positions have been on paths of political and academic collision. That is a good thing because the progress of human thought benefits from the encounter between adversaries. However, these encounters were often so politicized, so ill informed, and more ideologically than rationally inspired, that the overall outcome has not been especially productive.

We need to move beyond this stalemate. Not necessarily to achieve academic consensus but to creatively address the core issue: how to implement—worldwide—the basic insight that communication is inherent to human life. In the international community, we have hardly begun to reflect on what social, economic and cultural ramifications are at stake once we accept that without the entitlement to participation in societal communication processes; human life is at serious risk. This much-needed reflection has to liberate us from the mental cage from where we tend to conceive of communication as a transmission process rather than as a dialogical experience.

We have to identify the basic capacities humans should have in order to communicate and to discover the responsibilities and pleasures of human communication. There is still a long way to go but now we do have a good guide with us in the book of Aliaa Dakroury. This is a timely book worth reading, studying, and using in teaching on our contemporary communication realities.

Cees J. Hamelink

Professor Emeritus
University of Amsterdam
Amsterdam, February 2009

Chapter 1

Introduction: Is Communication a Basic Human Right?

The above question reflects my desire, beyond the time spent in researching and writing this book, to respond to what I have always perceived as an increasing need in the field of communication studies: a new and unique perspective on the importance of communication in relation to human rights.

One of the motivators behind this desire, that many are all too familiar with, stems from the daily complaints and media alerts from different email lists, messages that most would just delete or relegate to a spam filter of junk mail inbox. Who cares about a Chinese lawyer that has been jailed for three years for just forwarding an email about freedom of speech in China, which he received from an American friend? Who cares about these laws and regulations in many places in our world that forbid newspapers to publish their own opinions for the sake of political stability and good relationship with "friendly" countries? Who cares about editorials pulled from print simply because they do not conform to conglomerate media guidelines and policies? The many stories and alerts on arresting bloggers for posting their opinions online; Internet censorship; governments shutting down websites; surveillance of online forums, are only a few on a very long list on instances where human communication is not freely practiced, if not completely violated.

These strong words of "electronic colonization," "technological imperialism," "Western domination," "imbalanced flow of information," etc., are also among the triggers in realizing the importance of the relationship between communication and human rights. They motivated me to ask more questions, inducing a desire to know "WHY"? Why did people complain about these cases? One could argue that freedom of speech, expression, and thought are not as important as food, air, or water, but they are undoubtedly necessary for human existence.

A strange but interesting reason that sparked the idea behind this book was one of the various conversations and discussions I had with one of my colleagues. He told me that his daughter sometimes complained about following the rules and she kept asking him: "why should I go to sleep early? I have a right to watch television late!" This conversation caused me to contemplate the concept of a "right" as one of our daily discourses, pondering whether it would be valuable and interesting to clarify the definition of a "right" and why it is so desirable to human beings. Further, would it be even *more* valuable and interesting to know if communication could be one of those rights?

The relationship between communication and human rights is not a recent idea. It is a core ideal rooted in the historical contributions of the early Greek philosophers. In exploring this proposed relationship, it is imperative to look closely at the concepts of "justice" and "freedom" in the works of Plato and Aristotle specifically to establish a foundation for the ethics of communication as a human right. The Greeks introduced many concepts which are integral to the language of human rights today, among them democracy, justice, freedom, and equality, thus planting the seeds of our modern human rights. The philosophers debated these rights within contextual authority of the time, developing "*isogoria*, or equal freedom of speech, and *insonomia*, which implied equality before the law" (Palumbo, 1982: 14, *emphasis in original*). Even Greek rulers and statesmen allowed for a democracy where varying opinions could flourish in the public sphere and where philosophers could discuss their ideas and debate freely and without oppression. This idea is clear in the writing of philosophers such as Socrates, Plato, and Aristotle, who were concerned about ethics and moral rules and how to achieve "justice" in order to create the "ideal society."

In *The Republic*, Plato discusses one of the fundamental principles of the human rights issue: "justice." In one of the dialogues, Socrates states that justice "is, as you know, sometimes spoken of as the virtue of an individual, and sometimes as the virtue of a State" (cited in Fireman, 1957: 4). An interesting point made in the discussion of "freedom of speech" in *The Republic* is that a certain degree of censorship of information is predictable, and even *acceptable*, in order to ensure that rhetorical activities that could deceive the public are controlled. In explaining this point, Fireman writes, "Literature here is the main worry of Plato as it deals with all mythological tales and religious narratives, which are most frequently quite false: all poets are careless about the truth. Hence a censorship will be established to pass on which tales are good and which are bad, and then even mothers and nurses will have to tell only the authorized stories" (Ibid: 20).

Importantly, we have to consider the centrality of "truth" for Plato. At the heart of his philosophy lies a major distinction between "philosophy" and "rhetoric." For Plato, philosophy is the only activity that leads to the truth; rhetorical discourses—such as writing books or making speeches—would not lead to truth, only to arguments and dialectics. Another central issue for Plato is achieving a degree of metaphysical thought that reveals a divine-human relationship, represented by "winged words." Plato asserts the importance of these winged words (oral discourse) as the seeds of love and the soul-to-soul relationship. The importance of "orality" in his philosophy justifies why he allowed controlled censorship of "untruthful" and "deceptive" oral activity (Fisher, 1966). Looking at it in this way, one could argue that Plato was among the pioneers who attacked and criticized the seeds of "propaganda" in Greek society as a manipulative method of persuasion.

Equally important to mention here is the contribution of the Stoics of ancient Greece to the idea of "natural law," a concept which is central to the principles of human rights. They believed that "justice" is a transcendent quality, linking humans to the divine, and that this relationship should bring all men into a relationship of brotherhood. They did not deny the difference between themselves, Greeks, foreigners, or barbarians, and the slaves in their own public sphere, far away from authorities and political institutions (Ibid: 14–16).

Inspired by the Greek School of the Stoics, the great Roman jurist Marcus Tillius Cicero (106–43 A.D.) developed another conception of natural law, or *jus naturale*, in his many writings. Even though there is no mention of the term "communication" in Cicero's *Brotherhood of Man*, we can understand that what he is claiming[1] is certainly communication in the sense discussed previously. Most interesting is his conception of communicative actions as basic natural rights for all humans. How Cicero articulated the right to communicate can be seen in his use of words or phrases such as "as apply to all," "prove and disprove," "discuss," "imprinted on our minds," and "speech, the mind's interpreter," which refer to discussion and interaction, freedom of speech, verbal and non-verbal messages, freedom of thought and the intellectual copyrights that are included in the *Universal Declaration of Human Rights* (UDHR) of 1948. Interestingly, they are commonly held discourses in the present day especially with the rise of new technologies such as the Internet.

In addition to the Greek and Roman contributions to theorizing communication as a human right, an examination of the cultural and religious traditions and practices of Judaism, Christianity, and Islam is also necessary as many have argued that they have nourished the idea of human rights generally and the Right to Communicate specifically. This argument contradicts, to a great extent, the idea of the Western origin of human rights. When dealing with the origin of human rights ideals in Judaism, Christianity, and Islam, one can argue that although the principles of human rights existed within the practice and tradition of these religions, the process of "languaging" communication as a human right emerged only recently within the Western tradition.[2] Froman explains that in societies there are advantages for those who are able to impose a certain "language" over other languages; therefore "those to whom advantages go will enforce language which promotes and protects those advantages. This requires control over the institutions in that society. . . . None of the 'normal' institutions of a society, then, will advocate the establishment of new vocabularies if the language would change the structure of advantages" (1992: 11).

The principles of Judaism, for example, date back to the Hebrews and their practices: As Palumbo tells us, "[They] were among the first to put into practice a policy of respect for the dignity of every individual" (1982: 13). Judaism, especially in the Old Testament, embodies the principles of "justice" and "mercy" for both the Jew and the outsider, as stated in Leviticus: "You shall have one law for the stranger and citizen alike: for I am the Lord your God" (Ibid). Christianity also expresses the idea of human rights through two main principles: universality and immortality of soul. Firstly, like Plato and his notion of *Eros* or love, Jesus taught his message of love to everyone, to the multitudes—in Peters' words, "just like broadcasting" (2001: 59–62). Central to Christianity is the idea of immortality of the soul, clarified as the "doctrine [that] lays emphasis on each man's importance and worth as an individual. Every human being was created by God and is destined for eternal life. This being the case, each person has the right to be treated with respect because he is more than a cog in a wheel but a special and unique creation of God" (Palumbo, 1982: 17).

Finally, we find the idea of human rights expressed in the Islamic principles drawn from the Muslim *Qur'an*, the Word of God, considered as Islamic law (or *Shari'ah*), and the Prophet's practice (*Sunnah* or *Hadith*)—a collection of the Prophet's principles and practices as recited by his companions. Basically, the roots of equality in Islam go back to the creation of human beings: all human beings are equal, as they are all the children of Adam. In addition to the moral and ritual practices of human rights in Islam, the right to communicate has also been addressed. In 1981, the *Universal Islamic Declaration of Human Rights*[3] was ratified and adopted by all Muslim countries. It contains 23 articles that include, for example, the right to life, freedom, and equality and prohibition against impermissible discrimination; justice, fair trial, protection against abuse of power, freedom of belief, thought and speech . . . among others (Ali, 2000: 28–30).

Interestingly, Article (12)[4] covers the freedom of belief, thought, and speech, which is related to the Platonic moral right to apply a limited censorship of "rhetorical" or false words that could deceive the public. In addition, Mayer asserts Article (22) "invites censorship in accordance with Islamic criteria or on the grounds of Islamic morality, . . . [it] provides that there is a right to express opinions freely—but only in a manner not contrary to the principles of the *shari'a* [*Shari'ah*]" (1991: 77). These positions are very significant as they constitute both the philosophical and "ethical" basis for discussing communication as a human right on the one hand, and, on the other, represent a foundationalist position of conceptualizing a right.

In England in 1215, the greatest and oldest hallmark of human rights treaties, the *Magna Carta*, was issued when a group of English nobles forced King John to sign the document that is today considered the first official or formal "language" of human rights. Bradley says that this document was initially a confrontation between the barons (which represent a major power during this time) and the king, containing many details about the "feudal system" which existed in the thirteenth century (2001: 5–7).

Observing this treaty, we notice two main points, the first being the kind of communication that existed between the barons and English nobility, and the second being the way this document is "languaged." As for the first point, and taking into consideration the historical fact that during the thirteenth century Kings had massive power to neglect public rights that varied from the right to life, property, freedom, and others on the one hand, the public sphere resisted these powers and denied them. Despite the fact that nobles and barons forced the King to sign this document, the public was accepting and supportive of their actions, even if non-verbally. Given that "language is reality creating," and the tools of language are many—among them words—which "make things exist and give them appearances" (Froman, 1992: 4–5), we can see the way this treaty gave appearance to the ideal of human rights through even the language used. Along with many following treaties, declarations, and covenants, *Magna Carta* used the term (man) but in an imperative tone to forbid any kind of violations to his right. For example, it mentioned in its clauses the words: (no free man), (no man), (any man), (without), and (whatever). In other words, without using this language of imperative and forbiddance—such as "no," "no one," "any," . . . etc. to intertwine with human rights, there will be no awareness of its existence in the first place, and hence, no guarantee of its enforcement and enhancement.[5]

At this point, the reader may be questioning what is so special about my interpretation of intellectual history since tens, hundreds, or maybe even thousands of scholars have dealt with these philosophers, including Milton, Locke, Mill, and Habermas. I believe I have brought to light important features of communication that have not been sufficiently discussed, through the historical foundation of the concept of communication as a human right. With our rapid modernization and development of communication media, it becomes increasingly important to conceptualize a "right" and to pay greater attention to the individual and societal responsibilities associated with it.

I view my effort as a primary academic clarification of dealing with communication as a human right. Unless there is an established, clear, intellectual and philosophical understanding of this concept it can hardly be possible to successfully navigate the waters of the daily practices of communication. The fundamental question necessary to answer in order to achieve this understanding is: What are the practices that could be "rights" and deserve to be backed by various declarations?

Is communication a basic human right? This is the main question articulated in this book and has provided the organizational framework on which this research was conducted. In Chapter 2, "Early Context of the Right to Communicate," an analysis of the historical declarations that support the international recognition of the concept of the Right to Communicate are explored, including the American Declarations, the French Declaration, the Universal Declaration of Human Rights, and the United Nations Educational, Scientific and Cultural Organization (UNESCO) Media Declaration. The chapter also investigates the international flow of information debates, especially during the work of the MacBride Commission that nourished the idea of treating communication as a human right.

Following that, this book points out the great controversies that emerge, and the problems that are raised from treating communication as a universal and absolute right to be bestowed upon all human beings "without qualification." In Chapter 3, "A Debate on What Is a Right to Communicate," examples of these claims can be seen in the heated debates surrounding totalitarianism and propaganda, hate speech versus free speech, the Internet, pornography, and offensive signs, invasion of privacy and the Right "Not" to Communicate, and problems arising from media ownership and control. For that, I propose a provisional conceptualization of a "right," by questioning its creation, causes, and possibilities, concluding the importance of maintaining a reciprocal relationship between rights and duties or responsibilities.

Following this, I am proposing a historical clarification of intellectual contributions to this concept, and what they could possibly offer to answer the core question of the book in Chapter 4, "Philosophical Foundation of Communication as a 'Human Right'." It starts with the seventeenth century thinker John Milton and his understanding of communication as a "uni-dimensional" right, followed by the English philosopher John Locke and his assertion on the absolute individual freedom. Highlighting an attempt to view communication as a human right from a legal perspective, this chapter discusses the work of the Baron de Montesquieu through his legal realization of liberties, followed by analyses of the absolute freedom of speech as advocated by French philosopher Voltaire. In the last section of this chapter, the ideas of two key philosophers are discussed and linked to a possible Right to Communicate through the work of Jeremy Bentham, especially his standpoint on public opinion and freedom of expression, followed by John Stuart Mill and his view of an absolute right relative to greatest happiness.

In Chapter 5, "Toward a Theorization of Communication as a 'Human Right'," the focus moves to a critical reflection and a proposal to theorize the Right to Communicate by drawing a link between the standpoints of early intellectuals and more contemporary theorists arguing that John Dewey, Jürgen Habermas, and Herbert Schiller offer examples of a more plausible understanding of communication as a human right. In particular, this chapter analyzes the concept of "communication" from Dewey's viewpoint as a genuine social dialogue and not merely the sending and receiving information. It also dissects the Habermasian belief in "undistorted" communication. In trying to situate the argument within the context of the concurrent research on the Right to Communicate, the last section of this chapter underlines one possible way to conceptualize communication as a human right through the work of Herbert Schiller and his particular emphasis on Right to Communicate "cultures." Nonetheless, Schiller was personally involved in the work of the MacBride Commission and the evolving concept of the Right to Communicate.[6]

In Chapter 6, "The Question of the Right to Communicate," I repose the question of treating communication as a human right, and striving for a workable answer, argue that the evolution of the Right to Communicate has evolved historically in three different phases. The first phase was through the various legal declarations and documents, viewing them as merely the "language" answer to the main question articulated in the book. In the second phase—the realization—the Right to Communicate surfaced in many international debates, asserting the importance of communication as a human right in various international discourses, notably the MacBride Commission. Finally, the aim of part three—the practice phase—is to discover the different cases we commonly encounter when dealing with communication in real life that vary from the extreme authoritative type to a responsibility model.

Generally, in trying to situate the argument of this book within the context of the concurrent research on the Right to Communicate, this book aims to underline the historical, intellectual, philosophical, and theoretical roots of communication as a human right. The main argument here is that, although there is indeed an *implicit* relationship between the Right to Communicate and the previous literature and research in this field of study, the study of communication lacks an *explicit* link between the fields of communication and human rights.

Notes

1. In his *Brotherhood of Man,* Cicero maintained: "We may define man, a single definition will apply to all. This is sufficient proof that there is no difference in kind between man and man; for if there were, one definition could not be applicable to all men; and indeed reason which alone raises us above the level of the beasts and enables us to draw inferences, to prove and disprove, to discuss and solve problems, and to come to conclusions is certainly common to us all and though varying in what it learns, at least in the capacity to learn it is invariable" (cited in Palumbo, 1982: 130).

2. This point raised the issue of universality versus the locality of human rights, which is represents one of the heated debates in studying human rights.

3. The Universal Islamic Declaration of Human Rights' preamble states: "Whereas Allah (God) has given mankind through His revelations in the Holy *Qur'an* and the *Sunnah* of His Blessed Prophet Muhammad an abiding legal and moral framework within which to establish and regulate human injustice; . . . do hereby, *as servants of Allah and as member of the Universal Brotherhood of Islam, . . . affirm our commitment to uphold the following inviolable and inalienable human rights that we consider are enjoined by Islam*" (Ali, 2000: 291, *emphasis in original*).

4. Article (12) asserts: "a) Every person has the right to express his thoughts and beliefs so long as he remains within the limits prescribed by the law. No one, however, is entitled to disseminate falsehood or to circulate reports which may outrage public decency, or to indulge in slander, innuendo or to cast defamatory aspersions on other persons. b) Pursuit of knowledge and search after truth is not only a right but a duty of every Muslim" (cited in Ali, 2000: 293).

5. One clause states: "NO FREE MAN shall be taken or imprisoned, or be dissiesed of his freehold, or liberties, or free customs, or be outlawed, or exiled, or any other wise destroyed: nor will we pass upon him, nor condemn him, but by lawful judgment of his peers, or by the law of the land. We will sell to no man, we will not deny or defer to any man either justice or right." And in another: "that no man of whatever estate or condition that he be, shall be put out of land or tenement, not taken, any imprisoned, nor disinherited, nor put to death, without being brought in answer by due process of law" (Bradley, 2001: 6).

6. His submission to the MacBride Commission appears in the Betty Zimmerman's collection, which was donated to the School of Journalism and Communication, Carleton University, Ottawa. Zimmerman was the Canadian representative in the MacBride Commission, replacing famous Canadian communication theorist Marshall McLuhan. She was also the only female member in the Commission.

Chapter 2

Early Context of the Right to Communicate

Congress shall make no law respecting an establishment of religion, or prohibiting the free exercise thereof; or abridging the freedom of speech, or the press; or the right of the people peaceably to assemble.

American Bill of Rights, 1789

The unrestrained communication of thoughts and opinions being one of the most precious rights of man, every citizen may speak, write, and publish freely, provided he is responsible for the abuse of this liberty, in cases determined by the law.

Declaration of the Rights of the Man and of the Citizen, 1789

> Everyone has the right to freedom of opinion and expression; this right includes freedom to hold opinions without interference and to seek, receive and impart information and ideas through any media and regardless of frontiers.
>
> *Universal Declaration of Human Rights*, 1948
>
> Everyone shall have the right to freedom of expression; the right shall include freedom to seek, receive and impart information and ideas of all kinds, regardless of frontiers, either orally, in writing or in print, in the form of art, or through any other media of his choice.
>
> *International Covenant on Civil and Political Rights*, 1966

As illustrated above, communication, or some aspect thereof, has often been included in formal declarations of human rights. In many cases, its status as a basic human right has been considered "unproblematic," "taken-for-granted," and "unquestionable." Before examining some of the problems that actually arise from according communication this status, it will be helpful to consider the nature and context of some of the most important of these formal documents of communication as a human right; in particular, the *American Bill of Rights*, 1789, the *Declaration of the Rights of the Man and of the Citizen*, 1789, the *Universal Declaration of Human Rights*, 1948, the *International Covenant on Civil and Political Rights*, 1966, and the UNESCO *Media Declaration*, all of which state that communication is, universally, one of the "basic" human rights.

During the eighteenth century, America (followed by France) made formal declarations of human rights that actually served as tools for limiting the power of legislatures and legal institutions rather than for expressing inherent liberties and freedoms. Reid has observed, "rights in the eighteenth century were thought of as restraining arbitrary government rather than as liberating the individual. . . . [The] concept of rights was torn between the ideal of freeing human subjectivity and the reality of confining human subjectivity within the mores of a customary society" (1986: 73).

American Bill of Rights

Drawing from the language of eighteenth century philosophy, the *Virginia Declaration* of June 12th, 1776, the *Declaration of Independence*, July 4th, 1776, and the *American Bill of Rights*, 1789, appeared to place great emphasis on freedom through the use of phrases such as "by nature free," "inherent rights," "enjoyment of life and liberty," "no men be deprived of this liberty," "unalienable right," and "pursuit of happiness." For example, Article (1) of the *Virginia Declaration* stated:

> That all men are by nature equally free and independent, and have certain inherent rights, of which, when they enter into a state of society, they cannot by any compact deprive or divest their posterity; namely, the enjoyment of life, liberty, with the means of acquiring and possessing property, and pursuing and obtaining happiness and safety.

In Article (12) of the same Declaration, the following was added:

> That the freedom of the press is one of the great bulwarks of liberty, and can never be restrained but by despotic governments.

Finally, Article (1) from the *American Bill of Rights* specifies the freedom of the press as part of the basic rights:

> Congress shall make no law respecting an establishment of religion, or prohibiting the free exercise thereof; or abridging the freedom of speech, or the press; or the right of the people peaceably to assemble.

The ambiguity surrounding rights was, and still is, one of the controversial issues that is raised when we discuss the right to communicate historically, especially the freedom of the press. Obviously, these Articles conclude that the freedom of the press was one of the basic "legal" rights to be enforced and maintained by the American Congress, rather than consider it as an absolute "right" to communicate. In other words, legal judgment and constitutional laws bind the freedom of the press, and the goodness of freedom is determined by their consequences, for example, whether they are good or bad for the status quo. Therefore, individuals do not have the full liberty to exercise communication the way they want, but according to what the laws permit them to do.

Consequently, it can be argued here that in eighteenth century America, despite the prevalence of liberalism, communication (in the sense of freedom of the press) was a regulated activity, following laws and constitutional regulations more than expressing autonomous individual rights. The following summary defines how the American revolutionaries understood the freedom of the press:

> The liberty of the press is indeed essential to the nature of a free state: but this consists in laying no previous restraints upon publications . . . to forbid this, is to destroy the freedom of the press; but if [an individual] publishes what is improper, mischievous, or illegal, he must take the consequence of his own temerity. [T]o punish (as the law does at present) any dangerous or offensive writings, which, when published, shall on a fair and impartial trial be adjudged of a pernicious tendency, is necessary for the preservation of peace and good order, of government and religion, the only solid foundations of civil liberty. Thus the will of individuals is still left free; the abuse only of that free will is the object of legal punishment.
>
> (Reid, 1988: 118)

This historical context leads to the assumption that the American *Declarations* are not the basis of a Right to Communicate, but rather, they can be merely considered as "statements" of some legal enforcement and protection of the "freedoms" of speech and press, as types of communication.

Even if the American Revolution historically precedes the French, many scholars argue that, in many ways, the French Revolution represented a more radical social change than the American, especially for the realization of the ideals of democracy and freedom as well as for the realization of the Right to Communicate, which embodies freedoms of speech, expression and so on. This idea may be due to the radical changes effected by the French Revolution on the beliefs, structures and policies of the society. The Declarations spawned by the American Revolution are conceived as extensions of the *Magna Carta* and the English *Bills of Rights*; as a former British colony, America's main aim in the Revolution was independence from the British sovereignty. Costas Douzinas, in *The End of Human Rights: Critical Legal Thought at the Turn of the Century,* clarifies the distinction: "The aim of the American documents was to legitimize political independence from Britain, while that of the French, the overthrow of the social order of the *ancien régime*" (2000: 87). Moreover, Douzinas mentions that even the French parliament acknowledged the American Revolution in August 1789, but with "a sharp distinction between the two Declarations" (Ibid: 88).[1]

The French Revolution and *La Déclaration des Droits de l'Homme et du Citoyen*

French historian, François Furet, argues that it is important to recognize the genuine difference or contrast between the French and the American Revolutions. The American Revolution, he writes, was the "*non-revolutionary* establishment of democracy" (1998: 68, *emphasis in original*), as America had been settled by European immigrants who built a new society and rejected sovereign rule from afar to establish their own form of government based on the realization of the Enlightenment principles of individual rights and the sovereignty of the people.

> The American revolutionaries, it is true, also had to fight a certain number of their compatriots who rallied to the English cause. But the American republic, once it became independent, possessed only a single history, which served as a source of pride and unity.
>
> (Ibid)

In contrast, the aim of the French Revolution was to achieve a utopian ideal, and that purpose was characterized by its insistence on changing the old order—*l'ancien régime*—to create a new society, which was chartered in 1789 in *La Declaration des Droits de l'Homme et du Citoyen*. Jürgen Habermas, in his *Theory and Practice*, confirms this idea by arguing that, in the American Revolution, "it is a matter of setting free the spontaneous forces of self-regulation in harmony with Natural Law, while in [France, the Revolution] seeks to assert for the first time a total constitution in accordance with Natural Law against a depraved society and a human nature which has been corrupted" (Habermas, 1973: 105).

In fact, some scholars considered communication to be one of the primary motivators of the French Revolution. Baker, who adopts one perspective, argues that there was an interaction between three major competing political forces or discourses: the first is the discourse of "justice," the language of the French parliament and monarchic power; the second is the discourse of "will," the language of the public's desire for freedom and political reform; and finally, the discourse of "reason" and the legitimizing language of the Enlightenment ideology. In the end, the discourse of public defeated the other two discourses, resulting in the French

Revolution and democratic reform (2001: 70–74). Affirming this opinion, one could see that the type of communication that existed during the French Revolution played a significant role in asserting the discourse of free public will. Jill Maciak (2001), for example, reveals that the written media such as tracts and newspapers, along with the oral communication that reached the non-educated people in the villages and countryside through postmen, messengers from King, and rumours, played a key role in forming political public opinion during the French Revolution.

Furthermore, looking at the circulation of ideas and discourses in the context of the history of communication, it can be noted that publications (including journals, published books, pamphlets, and so on) also played a fundamental role in forming the public sphere and public opinion during the French Revolution; and that the transmission of philosophical, political and scientific texts had a powerful impact on the discourses of that time. Baker (2001: 64–65), looking at books as neither "objects," nor "isolated ideas," stresses the importance of the study of the pre-revolution circulation of texts and ideas within which the "political discourse" existed. He notes that society in that period was "unified" by the kind of written materials being circulated.

In his *The Forbidden Best-Sellers of Pre-Revolutionary France*, Darnton discusses the "Livres Philosophiques" as fanning the flames of the spirit of freedom and the need to reform, and fueling the desire to attain freedom of thought, speech and expression. These books, written by various philosophers and intellectuals such as Voltaire, Rousseau, and Mercier, among others, were extraordinarily popular. Darnton cites some opinions of that time that express the public's thirst for those texts:

> Never has one seen so many forbidden works as today. . . . No one is ashamed to be occupied with a bad book. . . . People are bent on getting . . . [forbidden books], no matter what the price.
>
> (2001: 116)

In addition to the books and periodicals, pamphlets were commonly used during this time as an easy and accessible medium of communication. Pamphlets could be used not only to criticize the government but also to defend it, thus serving as a way to air the advantages and disadvantages of a given policy such as taxes, for example. Books and pamphlets were extremely popular: "The pamphlets, too, were *libelles*—shorter, sharper, and more up-to-date versions of the stories that had circulated in book form" (Ibid: 137).

La Déclaration des Droits de l'Homme et du Citoyen, or the Declaration of the Rights of the Man and of the Citizen, was undeniably a turning point—especially in the history of the idea of treating communication as a basic human right—as it synthesized the Enlightenment concepts of "freedom," "liberty," and "fraternity" in expressing opinions and attitudes. It was the first formal realization of the right to "unrestrained" communication as a "sacred" right of human beings.

Before analyzing this Declaration and its Articles, it is interesting to note some historical facts that help to show how the American and French Declarations use similar language, despite their previously introduced historical and political differences. French Declaration was written by Marie-Joseph Paul Yves Roch Gilbert du Motier, Marquis de Lafayette (1757–1834), known as The Marquis de Lafayette[2], and was adopted by the French National Assembly in August 26th, 1789 (which had been occupied by Lafayette at the time). The Marquis de Lafayette was a French military leader who fought with the colonists during the American Revolution, as a volunteer. This is the reason behind his famously known title, "the hero of two worlds"—America and France. After his service in America, he was deeply affected by liberal thoughts and became one of the great French advocates for social reform. He supported the ideas of equality, liberty, and freedom, including the freedom of the press. Lafayette wrote the following in his memoirs, "At the age of nineteen, I gave myself over to the liberty of man and the destruction of despotism . . . I left for the New World, impeded by all and helped by none" (Lafayette, cited in Bernier, 1983: 196).

In January 1798, Lafayette wrote the first draft of the *Declaration of Rights,* and then showed it to his friend, the American Ambassador in France at the time, Thomas Jefferson (1743–1826), who was responsible for writing the American Declaration of Independence. Lafayette acknowledged Jefferson's contribution in this process in his memoirs:

> I also wrote a Declaration of Rights which Mr. Jefferson found so excellent that he demanded it be sent to General Washington; and that declaration will just about become the new catechism of our country.
>
> (Lafayette, Ibid)

The French *Declaration* combined the rights of both "man" and "citizen," in other words, civil and political rights. Examining first the preamble of this declaration, we find an indication of morality in the words, "the following *sacred* rights of men and citizens," and in Article (1) that illustrates the idea of natural rights:

> Men are born, and always continue, free and equal in respect of their rights. Civil distinctions, therefore, can be founded only on public utility.

In Article (2), the focus is on different aspects of freedom, liberty, and equity:

> The end of all political associations is the preservation of the natural and imprescriptible rights of man; and those rights are liberty, property, security, and resistance of oppression.

It is important to mention here that it is very obvious there exists an ambivalence in conceptualizing "rights." First,

Article (2) affirms clearly that rights are "imprescriptible," then, in the same line states and prescribes them as the rights to liberty, property, and so on, which is clearly contradictory. Also, the *Declaration* formally states in Article (11) the importance of an "unrestrained" and "free" communication for every man and citizen. It also mentioned different formats of communication (opinions and attitudes, etc.) and different media (speaking, writing, etc.):

> The unrestrained communication of thoughts and opinions being one of the most precious rights of man, every citizen may speak, write, and publish freely, provided he is responsible for the abuse of this liberty, in cases determined by the law.

The same contradiction exists elsewhere in the *Declaration*. For example, while stating in the beginning that communication should be "unrestrained," the same Article sets up some preconditions for this type of communication; that it should be limited to the legal formats and framework.

It is interesting to mention here that some historical facts and examples refute, to a great extent, what is languaged to be an "unrestrained" communication. Consider first Olympe de Gouges's contribution (1748–1793), in cognizance of women's rights in France through her *Déclaration des Droits de la Femme et de la Citoyenne,* 1891. She was a feminist writer during the French Revolution, who published her declaration to criticize and object to the claims of "universality," and "absoluteness" in the *Declaration of the Rights of Man and the Citizen*. She pointed out that these principles were not applied to women, and thus, in practice, the *Declaration* was contradictory and incomplete. Moreover, even if the French advanced realization of rights is considered, the underestimation of the female's role and her equal rights to communication as a human being must also be analyzed. This fact was confirmed in the French National Convention in 1793, which declares that: "children, the insane, minors, women, and prisoners, until their rehabilitation, will not be citizens" (cited in Brems, 2001: 18). In other words, it is clear that the "sex" of the citizen was a significant barrier in applying French *Declaration's* principle concerning the "unrestrained" communication, representing a contradiction of the principles of the *Declaration* as well as highlighting the exclusion of women from the French public sphere during that time, as women were not allowed to be active participants in the public debates. Joan Wallach Scott argues that:

> The outcome of the French Revolution was contradictory: a universal, abstract, rights-bearing individual as the unit of national sovereignty, embodied, however, as a man. . . . [w]omen [have] to claim their political rights to be active citizens and, when denied them in practice, to protest against exclusion as unjust, a violation of the founding principles of the republic.
>
> (Ibid: 213)

Interestingly, in addition to equal rights to free speech and communication for men and women, de Gouges also claimed in her declaration for additional rights for women. Article (11) of her *Declaration* illustrates this point:

> The free communication of ideas and opinions is one of the most precious rights of woman, since this liberty guarantees that fathers will recognize their children. Any Citizen (citoyenne) can thus say freely: I am the mother of your child, without being forced by barbarous prejudice to hide the truth.
>
> (Scott, 2001: 222–225)

A staunch defender of human and women's rights, and a political activist whose writings and works were presented by the *Comédie Francaise*, Olympe de Gouges was sent in 1793 (even after the French Revolution and its *Declaration*) to the guillotine for plastering the walls of Paris with posters "urging that a federalist system replace Jacobin centralized rule" (Ibid: 234). Finally, the following was published to commemorate her:

> Remember that vigaro, that woman-man (cette femme-homme), the impudent Olympe de Gouges, who abandoned all the cares of her household because she wanted to engage in politics and commit crimes. . . . This forgetfulness of the virtues of her sex led her to the scaffold.
>
> (cited in Scott, 2001: 234)

Collectively, scholars confirm that, during this period, society was male-centered and women were neither considered as human beings nor as "men" who have rights. Instead, only men represented humanity in the *Declaration*. Douzinas (2000) quotes Joan Scoutt in *Only Paradoxes to Offer: French feminists and the rights of man*:

> Maleness was equated with individuality, and femaleness with otherness in a fixed, hierarchical, and immobile opposition (masculinity was not seen as femininity's other). The political individual was then taken to be both universal and male; the female was not an individual, both because she was non-identical with the human prototype and because she was the other who confirmed the (male) individual's individuality.
>
> (1996: 97)

A second example of the "unrestrained" communication is the case of "freedom of clothes." Adopting an interesting and novel perspective, Cissie Fairchilds explores, in a recent study, the freedom of expression during and after the French Revolution (after languaging the French *Declaration* that states the free and unrestrained types of communication) through an examination of fashions and clothes. She tells us that before the 1793 *French Convention of the Freedom of Dress*, the "right to free dress or outfit" was mainly a "privilege." Moved and inspired by the spirit of the Enlightenment principles and the philosophy of "natural rights," French citizens used their dress and outfits to express their opinions and attitudes, especially during the 1770s and 1780s. At that time, Fairchilds notes, dress no longer represented the social class; rather it expressed positions on political issues that were the subject of great debate during the revolutionary period. Some examples of this kind of creative expression were "hairdos depicting the Battle of Saratoga . . . [and in the] 1780s, for example, followers of the Duke d'Orleans, who favoured an English-style constitutional monarchy, proclaimed their allegiance by wearing English-style riding coats" (2000: 422).[3]

Paradoxically, while the 1793 Convention clearly states that freedom of dress is one of the basic human rights: "Everyone is free to wear whatever clothing and accessories of his sex that he finds pleasing" (cited in Fairchilds, 2000: 419). Yet, the second Article of the same Convention contradicts this right, as it requires populace to wear the same clothes: "The requirement that all French citizens wear a red, white and blue cockade in public" (Ibid). This case is an example of the explicit contradictions in this declaration, and what is really practiced in real life. Finally, French clothing, after 1797 up to present time, is not a method to distinguish man from citizen, but has become simply a personal freedom and method of communication.

In summary, the American and French rights of freedom of speech and of the press, as representative of the Right to Communicate during that time, can be summed up by the motto, "You are free to say what you want unless it is harmful or dangerous for the system." Interestingly, this idea is clearly languaged in the French *Declaration*, specifically in Article (4), and affirmed in Article (5):

> Political liberty consists in the power of doing whatever does not injure another. The exercise of rights of every man has no other limits than those

which are necessary to secure to every *other* man the free exercise of the same rights; and these limits are determinable only by the law.

. . .

The law ought to prohibit only actions hurtful to society. What is not prohibited by the law, should not be hindered; nor should anyone be compelled to that which the law does not require.

Languaging the *Universal Declaration of Human Rights*

The adoption of the *Universal Declaration of Human Rights* (UDHR) by the General Assembly of the United Nations on December 10, 1948, is considered to be the birth of the international recognition of human rights, including the Right to Communicate. Here, the main focus is on tracing to what extent this document has languaged the Right to Communicate, through a brief discussion of the languaging process, with a particular emphasis on Article (19), followed by a discussion of the current and important debate over the Right to Communicate.

First, it is useful to note that one of the most important purposes of the United Nations, as stated in the *United Nations Charter* of 1945 (preamble #2), is that it seeks to affirm its "faith in fundamental human rights"; and in Article (55-c) that it promotes a "universal respect for and observance of, human rights and fundamental freedoms for all without distinction as to race, sex, language, or religion" (cited in Brems, 2001: 20).

How the *Universal Declaration of Human Rights* came to be conceived and languaged during the first half of the twentieth century as a reaction to the events of pre- and post-World War II, and the heart-wrenching violations of human rights of that period, is a good starting point for the following discussion. The Nazis arguably carried out two of the worst mass human rights violations in history, before and during the Second World War[4], first by their genocide policy, and second by their denial of communication as one of the basic human rights. Different media such as newspapers, movies, cinemas, theatres, etc., were used by this totalitarian regime to disseminate ruling party ideology and propaganda, and to crystallize and polish the public image of the regime and its leaders. Media were forced to present only the "super heroic image" of their leaders. Moreover, violating freedom of communication on the inter-personal level, Nazi Germany forbade all types of communication between members of the public, i.e. no freedom of expression, no discussion of public policies, no exchange of views or opinions, no meetings, no expression of opposing views, no protests, etc.[5]

At the same time, books and other cultural materials were sanctioned; for instance, the Nazis burnt huge massive amounts of literature—including the works of Sigmund Freud—a situation that led many German writers, philosophers, and thinkers, especially those of Jewish origin, to leave Germany. Also, the Nazis burned many works of art, including paintings by Picasso, Van Gogh, etc. Both individual communication and mass media were heavily censored without any consideration for the right to know, or the right to information. Instead, the "population was fed a steady diet of propaganda" (Palumbo, 1982: 65).

First, arguments made that the *Universal Declaration of Human Rights* 1948, represents a largely Western cultural and philosophical perspective, not only in the reflection of Enlightenment ideals, but also in that the establishment of the *Universal Declaration of Human Rights* was mainly a reaction to President Franklin Roosevelt's speech in 1941 calling for the protection of "the four essential freedoms: freedom of speech and expression, the freedom of worship, the freedom from want, and the freedom from fear" (Morsink, 1999: 1).

"Drafters of the Universal Declaration wrote these freedoms in their Preamble," Morsink tells us, as a "tribute to this American president and his ideals" (Ibid).

The drafting of the *Universal Declaration of Human Rights* is a story that involves many players[6], roles, circumstances, debates, histories, and backgrounds. In order to relate this story, it is necessary to begin with the background, that is, the impact of eighteenth century ideals and views, where, it is argued here, the roots of communication as a human right can be found. Then, the contributions of the key players in the story, the drafters of the *Universal Declaration of Human Rights*, can be highlighted. Finally, the discussion centers on the debate over the languaging of the Declaration, and the narration of universality.

First, it is important to consider the impact of the Enlightenment, and in particular, the idea that all human beings are born "free" and that no one should restrain or violate this freedom or right. These principles were stated first in the *Virginia Declaration*, 1776, the *Declaration of Independence*, 1776, and the *French Declaration* of 1789, and now are enshrined in the UDHR in 1948. A strong reflection of these ideals is found in the words "freedom," "equal," "inalienable," "all," "justice," "natural," etc. in the preamble of the declaration, which are, as previously discussed, expressions that are found in the same language in the preambles of the three earlier declarations:

> Whereas recognition of the inherent dignity and of the equal and inalienable rights of all members of the human family is the foundation of freedom, justice and peace in the world.

Moreover, the constant use of the term "everyone" in the thirty Articles of this *Declaration* was another point of contention, as many delegates felt that the concept of "everyone" represented Western ideas and the belief in individuality, but not the social reality or collectivity of other cultures or their philosophies.

Article (19)

> Everyone has the right to freedom of opinion and expression; this right includes freedom to hold opinions without interference and to seek, receive and impart information and ideas through any media and regardless of frontiers.

Phrasing the Right to Communicate—as stated explicitly in Article (19) of the *Universal Declaration of Human Rights*—was subject to many efforts, proposals, and amendments, each represented by a different party with a different perspective and ideology. Among these efforts was the creation of a Sub-Commission, drawn from the Human Rights Commission, which was devoted to the discussion of freedom of information. This was especially important after the Second World War, considering the huge amount of propaganda that had been published from totalitarian regimes. In fact, one of the most important debates that occurred during the drafting of the *Universal Declaration of Human Rights* was raised by the delegation from the USSR[7], which questioned whether the Nazis had the right to communicate or not, considering that Hitler, after coming to power, abolished the constitutional laws and ruled instead through "emergency decrees" that were nothing but a series of human rights violations, including the violation of the freedoms of speech, movement, life, and property, among many others. These decrees empowered the government to "shut down the presses of the left-wing parties . . . to break up campaign rallies, to arrest opponents at will, . . . [and] also annulled almost all the basic rights guaranteed by the constitution" (Morsink, 1999: 65). They asked the Committee, therefore, to state this limitation and to include it in the Article. The Soviet delegation added: "The freedom of speech and the press should not be used for purposes of propagating fascism, aggression and for provoking hatred as between nations." The drafting commission rejected all these amendments that would deny full rights of communication to the Nazis with a vote of 23 to 10, with 13 abstentions. In the final wording of Article (19), the phrases "from sources wherever situated" and "to all channels of communication" were replaced by "through any media and regardless of frontiers" at the end of the Article.

What happened in the final moments of languaging the right to communicate is worth considering here. Humphrey says that on the night of December 10, 1948, the Ambassador of Soviet Union, Andrei Vishinsky, gave a speech explaining the reasons for his country's abstention. One of these reasons was related to Article (19). The Declaration had failed to articulate this right in such a way as to solve the problem of the usage of communication during wartime according to fascist principles, he stated, and argued further that:

> There could be no freedom of information unless the workers had the means to voice their opinions, and that meant having at their disposal printing presses and newspapers; the right to demonstrate in the streets should have been guaranteed; there were no guarantees that scientific research would not be used for war purposes; and there were no provisions protecting the rights of minorities.
>
> (Humphrey, 1984: 72)

The preceding discussion of the *Universal Declaration of Human Rights*, its importance and language, can be summarized here in the words of Eleanor Roosevelt from her speech on the occasion of the introduction of the *Universal Declaration of Human Rights* to the United Nations. Here she affirms the synthesis of the historical origins of the *Declaration*—the contributions of the great English, French, and American declarations:

> We stand today at the threshold of a great event both in the life of the United Nations and in the life of mankind, that is the approval by the General Assembly of the Universal Declaration of Human Rights recommended by the Third Com-

mittee. This Declaration may well become the international Magna Carta of all men everywhere. We hope its proclamation by the General Assembly will be an event comparable to the proclamation of the Declaration of the Rights of Man by the French people in 1789, the adoption of the Bill of Rights by the people of the United States, and the adoption of comparable declarations at different times in other countries.

(cited in Glendon, 2001: 166)

Beyond the *Universal Declaration of Human Rights*

In the second half of the twentieth century, many changes have occurred in the world. A significant change is the rise and development of modern media technologies, especially in the field of information and communication. Most significant, however, was the change in the social, economic, and political relations around the world, beginning with the founding of the Second World with the socialist countries, de-colonizing many countries, and the creation of the developing countries, or the Third World, and the existence of the developed countries or First World.

Here, the discussion focuses on an essential and relatively recent issue, that is, the concept of the "Right to Communicate" beyond the *Universal Declaration of Human Rights*. The origins of this right are illustrated first, followed by an explanation of the process of formal international languaging. Finally, the discussion includes the debate over this right, which leads up to its inclusion in the *UNESCO Media Declaration* of 1978.

For its origins, the concept of the "Right to Communicate," like the *Universal Declaration of Human Rights*, is the legal child of the international legal bodies, the United

Nations and UNESCO. The basis of the international recognition of communication as a human right, at least in language, was first stated in Article (19) of the *Universal Declaration of Human Rights* in 1948. It was then included, with slightly altered wording, in the *International Covenant on Civil and Political Rights* in 1966, which entered into force ten years later:

> Everyone shall have the right to freedom of expression; the right shall include freedom to seek, receive and impart information and ideas of all kinds, regardless of frontiers, either orally, in writing or in print, in the form of art, or through any other media of his choice.

There is a notable difference in the wording of this Article, eighteen years after the *Universal Declaration of Human Rights*: many new technologies had emerged since the post-WWII era in the world of communications, and "any other media of his choice" implies the future developments in this area. It is often argued that the two Covenants—the *International Covenant on Civil and Political Rights* and the *International Covenant on Economic, Social and Cultural Rights*—are two important international documents that complete the recognition of basic human rights. Their advantage lies in their statement of procedures for reporting and enforcing on human rights' status. From a communication standpoint, this covenant "receives greater weight than the . . . declaration, especially because [it] introduces essential specification to the freedom of information concept as understood in the Universal Declaration" (Nordenstreng & Hannikainen, 1984: 134).

Renewed interest in the terminology describing the rights of freedom of expression and access to information was initiated by Jean d'Arcy[8] in 1969, when he argued that the *Universal Declaration of Human Rights* along with the *International Covenant on Civil and Political Rights* were not sufficient to implement and inform what he termed the "right of man to communicate":

> The time will come when the Universal Declaration of Human Rights will have to encompass a more extensive right than man's right to information... This is the right of man to communicate... the angle from which the future development of communications will have to be considered.
>
> (Jean d'Arcy, 1969: 1)

It is useful here to present a brief chronological history of the right to communicate concept, as one of the basic arguments for treating "communication" as a fundamental and absolute human right. In fact, the history of this concept, which begins in the first half of the 1970s, as Richstad, Harms, and Kie (1977) explain, was initiated by the pioneering efforts of Jean d'Arcy, who launched his claim for the "right of man to communicate" in his famous article published in the *European Broadcasting Union Review* (EBU Review) in August 1969. As an advocate of human rights, Jean d'Arcy adopted a belief that humans cannot live without communicating with each other. "Man has a specific, a biological need to communicate," he said, and therefore, communication is one of the basic human rights. The principle applies to entire societies: "All societies spring from the communication" among their members, and if someone were to cut off this communication, then it is "equivalent to annihilating" that society (d'Arcy, 1982: 2).

Although Richstad, Harms, and Kie argue that he "did not specify in detail what he meant by the Right to Communicate . . . [his article] inspired others to attempt formulations over the following years" (1977: 114). They assert that historically, the *Canadian Broadcasting Act* (1968), was the next formal effort towards the realization of this right, especially the contribution of Henry Hindley, the Director of Telecommission Studies, who believed strongly, as the *Act* states, that "all Canadians are entitled to broadcasting service in English and French as public funds become available" (Ibid: 115). Following this *Act*, the Telecommission

Studies[9] task force formed by the Canadian Department of Communications produced a number of reports and studies regarding the issue of the right to communicate most notably the *Instant World* Report, 1971, that clearly defines the Right to Communicate:

> Freedom of knowledge and freedom of speech are among the most valued privileges of a democratic society. The rights to hear and be heard, to inform and to be informed, together may be regarded as the essential components of a "right to communicate" . . . the realization of a "right to communicate" is a desirable objective for a democratic society, so that each individual may know he is entitled to be informed and to be heard, regardless of where he may live or work or travel in his own country. The people of Canada—as a body and as individuals—are therefore entitled to demand access to efficient telecommunications services on a non-discriminatory basis and at a reasonable price.
>
> (*Instant World*, 1971: 3)

d'Arcy maintained that "at each step of human history, the formulation of law and the organization of social structures have been conditioned by the technology of communication," and he adds that these legal efforts are just an example of the "struggle of mankind for this right" (d'Arcy, 1977: 45). In fact, as Harms argues, the Right to Communicate, as defined since 1969, "differs from previous formulations to merit being called a new human right" (1982: 1).

UNESCO Media Declaration[10]

Certainly, from 1974 the Right to Communicate debate occupied a core part of the annual debate and argument of the

International Institute of Communications (IIC). As L. S. Harms documents, this concern led UNESCO to pay close attention to this concept and stress its importance in its programs, and in May 1978, the first official effort to language the right to communicate took place in a meeting of experts in Stockholm (1982: 1). Among the important facts that have influenced these international resolutions in general and this declaration in particular, is that 70 former colonies were decolonized during the 1960s, which brought about major political changes in power relations, with the existence of the non-aligned movement on the political side and the intellectuals' academic sphere on the other side. This change was among factors that played an important role in the 1969 UNESCO meeting of Experts on Mass Communication and Society in Montreal, Canada, which was followed by the Cologne, Germany 1975 conference of the IIC where the following resolution was adopted:

> Everyone has the right to communicate. [Communication] is a basic need and is the foundation of all social organization. It belongs to individuals and communities, between and among each other, the right has been long recognized internationally and the exercise of it needs constantly to evolve and expand.
>
> (Nordenstreng & Hannikainen, 1984: 294)

After this conference, there were several events where strong arguments were made for the importance of communication as one of the basic human rights and it was recognized that a full, international, and legal formulation was needed to uphold and enhance this right for the whole world.[11]

The UNESCO *Media Declaration* (1978) is considered in many ways to be the true turning point[12] in realizing and acknowledging that "communication" is a human capacity fundamental to our very existence.[13] This *Declaration* was adopted by the 146 UNESCO member states without any dissenting votes. The occasion was described as "not just another event of routine diplomacy but indeed a historical move" (Nordenstreng, 1984: 1). A close examination of this *Declaration* reveals some reinforcement of the Articles concerning free speech and communication previously proclaimed in the *Universal Declaration of Human Rights* and International Covenant on Civil and Political Rights, as well as other rights that are specific to this declaration. For instance, the Preamble states the following:

> Recalling the Universal Declaration of Human Rights, adopted by the General Assembly of the United Nations in 1948 and particularly Article 19 thereof, which provides that "everyone has the right to freedom of opinion and expression; this right includes freedom to hold opinions without interference and to seek, receive and impart information and ideas through any media and regardless of frontiers"; and the International Covenant on Civil and Political Rights, adopted by the General Assembly of the United Nations in 1966, Article 19 of which proclaims the same principles.

And Article (11) declares:

> For this declaration to be fully effective it is necessary, with due respect for the legislative and administrative provisions and the other obligations of Member States, to guarantee the existence of favourable conditions for the operation of the mass media, in conformity with the provisions of the Universal Declaration of Human Rights and with the corresponding principles proclaimed in the International Covenant on Civil and Political Rights adopted by the General Assembly of the United Nations in 1966.

In addition to the communication rights that are addressed in the passages above, new issues began emerging during the 1970s, such as the New World Information and Communication Order (NWICO), the Free Flow of Information, and journalists and media professional practices. As an example, Article (9) states the following:

> In the spirit of this Declaration, it is for the international community to contribute to the creation of the conditions for a free flow and wider and more balanced dissemination of information, and of the conditions for the protection, in the exercise of their functions, of journalists and other agents of the mass media. UNESCO is well placed to make a valuable contribution in this respect.

The Flow of Information Debate

It is useful to highlight other important historical events that fed into the debate on the need for the Right to Communicate within international communication policies beyond the various formal legal documents. Observers, advocates, and critics asserted that despite the decolonization of many countries after the Second World War, there was no clear evidence of their independence in real life. Schiller, for example, maintained that the idea of independence was an illusion, since American power was generally intertwined with the myth of the free flow of information that was carried by many international bodies, such as UNESCO, that ironically supported the imperialist powers while maintaining the status quo among the *"have-not"* nations.

> To believe that the commercial and informational points that join these economically feeble nations to the technologically powerful American economy are beneficial to both sides of the union is to outdo Voltaire's good doctor Pangloss. If free trade is a mechanism by which a powerful economy penetrates and dominates weaker one, the "free flow of information," the designated objective incidentally

of UNESCO, is the channel through which life styles and value systems can be imposed on poor and vulnerable societies.[14]

(Schiller, 1969: 52–53)

Following the Second World War, communication became an important aspect of the debate over the international flow of information, particularly in the 1960s as a result of the rapid growth of communication technology. During this period there was a growing need among the newly independent countries emerging in Asia and Africa to confront the "cultural legacy" of their former colonial relationships which manifested itself in many of the forms of political cooperation such as the Non-Aligned Movement (Hamelink, 1997: 70). This movement arose out of the 1955 Bandung Conference in which Asian, African, and Latin-American countries met to discuss first establishing and then developing economic links between the countries of the South. A major step in extending this cooperation into the cultural realm was the 1973 Non-Aligned Movement summit in Algiers, during which a clear opposition to the developmental paradigm in the field of communications began to emerge. The summit is considered to be the first evidence of a need to establish a *new international information order* to tackle the issue of cultural imperialism; indeed, it stated in its Economic Declaration that:

> It is an established fact that the activities of imperialism are not confined solely to the political and economic fields, but also cover the cultural and social fields, thus imposing an alien ideological domination over the peoples of the developing world.

(cited in Roach, 1999: 94)

At this point, it is important to consider the reasons that gave rise to what is termed *cultural imperialism*. Two significant changes occurred which can be considered as the underlying cause for the growing awareness of, and opposition to, cultural domination in the Third World, as well as its demand for the right to self-determination, not only in the fields of politics and economics, but also in the area of media and culture. The first of these events was the move from colonization to independence which occurred in many of these countries after WW II. Second, and perhaps of greater importance, were the efforts in this period of these newly independent countries to confront the spread of the communication developmental paradigm pioneered by Americans Daniel Lerner and Wilbur Schramm.

In his *The Passing of Traditional Society: Modernizing the Middle East* (1958), Daniel Lerner advocated for the idea of modernization by arguing that there is a major difference between traditional man (for example, those living in the developing countries), and modern man (those living in Western societies). He suggested that those in the West were no longer rejecting innovation and modernization, but were also beginning to question whether or not the modern lifestyles were workable. Furthermore, Lerner added that in order to achieve this phase of modernization, a society needs an efficient system of communication, "no modern society can function efficiently without a modern system of public communication" (Lerner, 1958: 213).

Support for this idea of Western superiority can be found in the work of Wilbur Schramm, particularly his *Mass Media and National Development: The Role of Information in the Developing Countries* (1964). In this book, he asserted that there is no way to escape from modernization; Schramm said bluntly about the under-developed countries that

> Unless they change, they will have to watch technological growth from the sidelines; social change will happen to them, rather than their playing an active part in bringing it about; they will be a part of the relatively inert mass out of which the leaders of development in their country are trying to fashion something "dynamic and vital."
>
> (Schramm, 1964: 19)

In this context, he added that modern communication, including technology, methods, and ideas, could be very powerful not only for developing Third World societies, but also for developing their cultures, adding that the highly developed countries have a much better supply of the various cultural and communication forms, such as radio, television, technical equipments, printing, recording, charts, and maps, among other media. In other words, he advocated the idea that "mass media are agents for social change" (Ibid: 114), since they are able to provide the means of transition from old customs and practices to substantially modern social relationships where "attitudes, beliefs, skills, and norms" are transformed into modern/Western forms. He also he added that this transformation is much easier "if it is not contrary to group norms"[15] (Schramm, 1964: 118).

In essence, Schramm argued that the mass media are able to create a climate for development by promoting investment and competitive operations that ultimately lead to the process of cooperation. In other words, mass media promote consumerism, which in turn promotes a climate of investment and competition, as opposed to totalitarianism which promotes monopolies. It should be noted that Schramm endorsed the Western capitalist model even in his communication analysis, where the adoption of capitalistic methods is tied into development and cooperation in the developing world. Secondly, he recommended that *"A developing country should review its restrictions on the importing of informational materials"* (1964: 264, *emphasis in original*).

Schramm noted that although the global trend at that time was to promote and exchange information within nations and countries, developing countries imposed certain rules on importing various cultural materials such as newspapers, films, textbooks, etc., through the imposition of national import taxes, and tariffs. Moreover, he questioned whether these developing countries, "with their great need for information, can afford such restrictions on the import of informational materials" (Ibid: 264).

Clearly influenced by the modernization/developmental discourse advocated by Daniel Lerner and Wilbur Schramm, the United Nations proclaimed the period 1961-1970 to be the "First United Nations Development Decade"[16] with the blanket assumption that Third World countries would best achieve development by adopting the same media, cultural, political, and economic forms that were found in the industrialized, ex-colonial Western powers. Such adoption would, it was believed; in turn transform these "developing" countries into more "developed" ones.

The MacBride Commission

International efforts started to emerge following the previously discussed debates highlighting the importance of the Right to Communicate, and warned of the dangers arising from the lack of the ability to practice that right. For example, in 1975 in Cologne, Germany, the IIC proposed that "Everyone has the right to communicate . . . the right has been long recognized internationally and the exercise of it needs constantly to evolve and expand" (Nordenstreng & Hannikainen, 1984: 294). Subsequently, there have been a number of international conferences stressing the importance of communication as one of the basic human rights, and pointing out that there needs to be full international regulatory formulas put in place to ensure that this right can be practiced in all countries, and not blocked or influenced by the "Northern" countries who own the means of communication (i.e., the technology). Examples of these efforts are the 1978 UNESCO Report on the Right to Communicate in Stockholm, the 1979 Manila Conference, UNESCO's 1980 Belgrade Conference, and the UNESCO General Conference in Paris 1983 (Nordenstreng & Hannikainen, 1984).

In the light of the previous discussion on the debate of modernization, the technique of transferring technology proved its inability to transform life in the Third World.

According to many observers and theorists[17], it was simply unsuccessful in representing the people's needs, hopes, and dreams in these regions, especially in the field of information and communications where "the primary beneficiaries (of telephony, educational television and satellite communications) have been foreign manufacturers, foreign bankers and national administrative and military elites" (Hamelink, 1997: 70). Yet, during the late 1970s, UNESCO as one of the United Nations' agencies, was a realm of heated debate between the minority Western countries, with their powerful resources and political forces[18], and the majority Third World countries with their powerful complaints and struggles.

Thus, within this international political environment, the 1976 UNESCO 19th General Conference in Nairobi recommended the establishment of a committee from a "reflexive group of wise men [to propose a] formula to resolve the conflict" (Ibid: 74). Chaired by the Nobel Peace Prize winner, Seán MacBride, the International Commission for the Study of Communication Problems was comprised of sixteen experts appointed in 1977 by the Director-General of UNESCO, Amadou Mahtar M'Bow, who noted that the committee's basic aim was to formulate possible ways to create a "freer and more balanced international flow of information and a more just and effective new world information order might be fostered" (Harley, 1993: 1).[19] The preliminary complaints investigated by the Commission were centered on Third World claims that there was: 1) an imbalance in the flow of news between the developed and developing countries; 2) that most of the news is controlled by the Western news agencies; 3) that Western news reporting is generally characterized by sensationalism and concentrates mainly on negative news stories when covering the non-Western regions; and most importantly, 4) that there is a Western dominance of ideas, information, and culture to the extent of threatening and disturbing the native cultures (Ibid: 7–8).

For this reason, the Commission produced eighty-two recommendations for fixing the existing global information order, and suggested policy changes that would make it possible to implement a human Right to Communicate. Recommendations 28, 29, and 30 were concerned mainly with the developing countries' right to communicate their identity, and culture. The Committee asserted that:

> *Promoting conditions for the preservation of the cultural identity of every society is necessary to enable it to enjoy a harmonious and creative inter-relationship with other cultures. It is equally necessary to modify situations in many developed and developing countries which suffer cultural dominance.*
>
> (Traber & Nordenstreng, 1992: 53, *emphasis in original*)

Here, one can see that commercialization of communications represented one major concern of the Third World. Therefore, it asserted that the different types of communications systems (such as TV, radio, and film, for example) should reflect the culture, traditions, and developmental objectives of the social and political national system in each country. Although these recommendations promoted the establishment of national cultural policies that would promote national identity in the developing countries, many critics believe that these were merely vague and non-workable recommendations. Herbert Schiller was one of those critics who maintained that the report was not effective in "dealing with the systematic patterns in the control of communication technology" (cited in Hamelink, 1997: 74–75).

Similarly, Hamelink added that another contradiction within the committee's recommendations was that in practice, national policies have not established a "national" identity; rather they are to a great extent promoting more "global than local culture, and that there are few indications of a more intensive cultural dialogue in the world" (Ibid: 80). Further, similar claims viewed the recommendations as a "disappointing" result that represented a failure to build a solid foundation for any future international communication order.[20] A NWICO was one of the main proposals in the MacBride Commission, including the assertion of the human Right to Communicate that had occupied several discussions in the UNESCO meetings. This argument defends the existence of the right to communicate as part of social justice and public interest principles.

> As resources become more complicated and more costly, the gap between the "haves" and the "have-nots" in the field of communications will grow. And since communications resources are an essential part of the infrastructure of developed communities, their availability is becoming progressively more important.
>
> (Harms, 1982: 18)

In the following years, this position represented a strong view point, espoused by advocates, researchers, and activists in the fields of communication and human rights especially with the involvement of Jean d'Arcy—the father of the Right to Communicate—during the proceedings of the MacBride Commission.

Chronologically, communication has been "stated" or "proclaimed" in various declarations and treatises from the eighteenth century until recent years, as a human right. The main question proposed here is: Does "stating" that communication is a basic human right make it so? Also, are there any possibilities for the existence of some problems that stem from treating communication as a "basic," "unproblematic," and "taken-for-grated" right? Accordingly, the next step is to explore or investigate the existence of the major problems and difficulties facing the unqualified assertion of "communication as a right."

Notes

1. See also Casey Harison who observes that the negative image of the French Revolution in the United States was the result of the American effort to "demonstrate the superiority of the American Revolution" (2002: 137).

2. It is interesting to mention here also, that he is the creator of the French modern flag.

3. Cissie Fairchilds quotes from one of the French Newspapers published during this period (*Journal Du Soir*, 30 April 1789) that supported the cancellation of mandated costumes: "Don't they know what influence exterior distinctions have on opinions . . . ? Don't they know yet that every time a man wears a uniform, he believes himself obliged to have opinions conforming to the dress that he wears?"(2000: 423).

4. Humphrey explains that prior to WWII, there was no legal awareness in the international community concerning human rights in general, and that these kinds of issues fell under the protection of national, state, or domestic law. The main reason for the "sudden concern" for human rights issues, he says, was "the traumatic experience through which the world had just passed. One of the causes of the Second World War was the cynical, studied and wholesale violation of human rights in and by Nazi Germany. This . . . was a war to vindicate human rights" (Humphrey, 1984: 5–12).

5. It must be noted here that even though democracy and liberty is practiced around the world in the twenty-first century, at least theoretically, the same violations of rights exist in many countries in particular circumstances, such war, crisis, or under emergency law. In many countries, emergency, and exceptional laws are enacted for many years, a situation that has given rise to

many advocates for the freedom of expression (among them IFEX, *International Freedom of Expression Exchange*, Index on Censorship, and Amnesty International, among others) appeal and demand to end this status and allow the process of free communication to occur. For more detailed documentation on the violations of freedom of expression around the world, see for example *www.ifex.org* and *www.article19.com*.

6. From the key drafters of the declaration: Eleanor Roosevelt, the widow of former U.S. president Theodore Roosevelt and a prominent figure and the chairman of the International Committee for drafting the *Universal Declaration of Human Rights*, Humphrey wrote in his diaries that she "was one of the greatest personalities ever to be associated with the United Nations, and her great prestige was one of the chief assets of the Human Rights Commission in the early years" (1984: 4). René Cassin, winner of the 1968 Nobel Peace Prize and the chief delegate of France, was another noticeable figure and an active participant in this process. Dr. Charles Malik, the head of the Lebanese delegation, a professor of philosophy at the American University in Lebanon, had received his Ph.D. from Harvard University where he was a student of the philosopher Martin Heidegger. Malik was one of the most active and influential contributors to the *Universal Declaration of Human Rights* drafting, thanks to his training in western philosophy and his belonging to a non-western culture.

7. Another position was taken by the Soviets, who clearly opposed upholding the "right to communication" for Fascists and Nazis, who, in their opinion, had manipulated the public using various media, including the press. Therefore they argued that "the world had just emerged from a terrible war, the objectives and scope of the press had changed and it was necessary to set limitations to the liberty of the press if it were used as a

vehicle of war propaganda and exhortation to revenge;" and claimed that the medium of the press, or any other media, should not be channeled by "anti-democratic" regimes that used propaganda.

8. Jean d'Arcy was the Director of Radio and Visual Services during the 1960s in the Office of Public Information at the United Nations in New York. President of the International Institute of Communications until his death in the 1980s, he was among the greatest advocates for the right to communicate. The article that sparked renewed debate was his 1969 "Direct broadcast satellites and the right to communicate" that appeared in the *European Broadcasting Union Review*.

9. In this regard, I have delved into the archival materials deposited in the National Archives of Canada to unveil the intellectual network established between the Canadian Telecommission Studies and Jean d'Arcy. In this exploration, it was confirmed by mutual correspondences between d'Arcy and Henry Hindley, the Executive Director of the Telecommission Studies, that d'Arcy was not only aware of their attempt, but interestingly praised it as a real novel approach to "apply" what was termed to as the Right to Communicate. It is important to note that the work of the Canadian Telecommission Studies started only one month after d'Arcy's launch of the Right to Communicate concept in the EBU review in August 1960. In Canada, September 1969, the Department of Communications announced the launch of the Canadian task force—known as the Telecommission studies—to examine and propose a telecommunications public policy to the Canadian government, enabling all Canadians to communicate freely and receive the telecommunication services on equitable and universal standards. Further, d'Arcy acknowledged that even the term the Right *not* to Communicate is a Canadian concept, developed by Henry Hindley during the International Broadcasting

Institute meetings during the mid-1970s, an idea that has garnered strong interest in recent years (i.e. privacy rights) (Dakroury, 2008).

10. The UNESCO Declaration on Fundamental Principles concerning the contribution of the Mass Media to strengthening Peace and International Understanding, to the promotion of Human Rights and to Countering Racialism, Apartheid and Incitement to war.

11. See, for example, the 1978 UNESCO Report on the right to communicate from the conference in Stockholm, another meeting in Manila 1979, the UNESCO 1980 Belgrade Conference, the 1981 conference in Strasbourg that adopted a resolution on the right to communicate, also the UNESCO General Conference in Paris 1983 (Nordenstreng & Hannikainen, 1984: 293–301).

12. Nordenstreng & Hannikainen observe, "It is a diplomatic miracle that such an outcome was possible in a case which had caused more controversy in UNESCO" (1984: 1).

13. It cannot be claimed that this declaration, though addressed to the media of communication, included all types of communication (i.e., inter-personal, personal, group, etc.); moreover, it concentrated mainly on the practice of journalism and problems of communication technology.

14. I think Schiller in this example was ironically using Voltaire's famous novel *Candide*, in which the character Doctor Pangloss (philosopher and teacher to the hero *Candide*) repeatedly uttered his famous rule that "all is for the best in this best of all possible worlds." Schiller suggested here that American imperialism is convinced, using the same rhetoric and practice, that what was good for America, would be good for the rest of the world.

15. For example, he argued that one of the barriers to modernization in the developing countries are their traditional religious beliefs: "Among such norms are the religious beliefs about fatalism and man's inability to do anything about nature, the taboos against killing living things no matter how dangerous to health and crops, the belief that hard work is demeaning, and the custom of going deeply into debt for weddings and dowries. It is impossible, in the process of modernizing, to avoid some confrontations with group norms. The question is, how to confront them" (Schramm, 1964: 118–119).

16. During this period, many Western governments and agencies generously sponsored a number of developmental projects in the south countries; most notable were the efforts of USAID (the United States Agency for International Development) which even now is one of the leading agencies in this area. However, such development is also the subject of some controversy over the imperialistic role of these agencies in the development of Third World countries (Thussu, 2000: 59).

17. Such as the work of Samir Amin (1976; 1977) for example.

18. Hamelink says that the Western minority tried to implement their general objectives which were: "[1)] avoid the adoption of a legally binding instrument on the demanded New International Information Order; [2)] to adopt a regulatory instrument only if it would reflect Western preferences; [and 3)] to maintain a consensus on the primacy of technical assistance in information matters" (1997: 72).

19. After the withdrawal of Marshall McLuhan due to a health condition, Betty Zimmerman joined the Commission to be the only female who contributed in such an important event.

20. It goes without saying that despite the Third World critiques of these recommendations, the Western response also expressed a general dissatisfaction and criticism of the commission's final reports. For example, the United States presented twenty seven pages of recommendations in this regard, claiming that the report was biased, and neglected the differing philosophies and standpoints of the other nations on the same issues (Harley, 1993: 92).

Chapter 3

A Debate on What Is a Right to Communicate

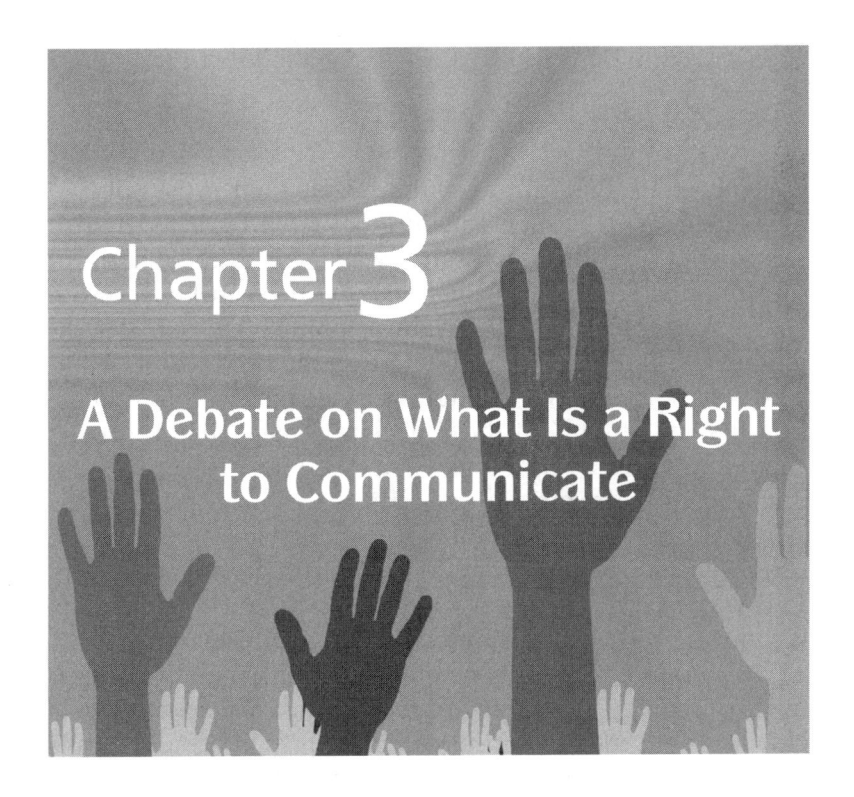

> The importance of keeping the conception of a right (or claim) and the conception of a privilege quite distinct from each other seems evident; and; more than that, it is equally clear that there should be a separate term to represent the latter relation. No doubt, . . . it is very common to use the term "right"; indiscriminately, even when the relation designated is really that of "privilege."
>
> *(Wesley Hohfeld, 1919: 14)*

It is argued that, despite the previously discussed formal declarations and international documents recognizing communication as one of the basic human rights, one could not deny that there are some difficulties and problems in applying this right on a universal and absolute scale. The following questions illustrate some of these problems. Do the Nazis have the right to communicate their racist political messages? Does Salman Rushdie have the right to publish *The Satanic Verses* even though it was deemed to be harmful to Muslims' feelings and beliefs? Even recently, does the Danish cartoonist have the right to publish cartoon[1] depicting the Muslim prophet Mohamed? Is the production of and access to pornography included in the right to communication that is "stated" in these declarations? What approach should be taken to hate speech on the Internet? Should the demand of child murderer Clifford Olson to publish his criminal memoir be considered on the basis of his right to communicate? Finally, how do journalists defend their right to free speech in the age of conglomerate media ownership, if communication is considered one of their human rights?

It is apparent from these questions that, though phrased in the language of universalism, the *Universal Declaration of Human Rights* fails to address some important issues. At the same time, it is important to recognize that if the Right to Communicate is to be considered an "inalienable" human right, it must be under specific circumstances and considered to be neither absolute nor universal. For example, in certain situations, such as the necessity of self-defence, a fundamental human right to life may be permissibly violated (Fisher, 1982: 17). To address these problematic questions, the following discussion considers whether the Right to Communicate is a basic, absolute, and primary human right available to all human beings at all times under any circumstances, as proclaimed in the international declarations and covenants; or whether it must at times be limited?

Totalitarianism and Propaganda

It is immediately obvious that acknowledging the Right to Communicate as an absolute and universal right could give rise to many problems and difficulties, such as the use of communication for propaganda purposes. Historically, as explained in Chapter 2, one of the main reasons for the international need to language human rights in general, and the Right to Communicate in particular, had to do with the inhumane practices of totalitarian regimes. It is clear that these regimes recognized the importance of the communication media in transmitting their propaganda and principles to the public. Yet, given Article (19) of the *Universal Declaration of Human Rights*, the question must be asked: do the Nazis have the right to communicate, to "seek," "receive" and "impart" information and ideas through "any media" and "regardless of frontiers"?

This case is very problematic, for if these or similar contemporary regimes possess this right, then the field of communication will be in chaos, subject to manipulation, and potentially harmful or dangerous to many people. It is interesting in this context to highlight and analyze the conception of communication according to some previous totalitarian regimes. For instance, Benito Mussolini, in one of his speeches, rejects the morals and ideals of the Enlightenment to assert the higher purpose of "collective will" over individuality, and attacks the concept of "natural law":

> Fascism sees in the world not only those superficial, material aspects in which man appears as an individual, standing by himself, self-centered, subject to natural law which instinctively urges him toward a life of selfish momentary pleasure; it sees not only the individual but the nation and the country; individuals and generations bound together by a moral law, with common traditions and a mission which suppressing the instinct for life closed in a brief circle of pleasure, builds up a higher life, founded on duty, a life free from the limitations of time and space, in which the individual, by self-sacrifice, the renunciation of self-interest, by death itself, can achieve that purely spiritual existence in which his value as a man consists.
>
> (cited in Palumbo, 1982: 173–174)

More interestingly, he also asserts the importance of the practice of these concepts through the media of language, customs and records:

> In the Fascist conception of history, man is man only by virtue of the spiritual process to which he contributes as a member of the family, the social group, the nation, and in function of history to which all nations bring their contribution. Hence the great value of tradition in records, in language, in customs, in the rules of social life. Outside history man is a nonentity. Fascism is therefore opposed to all individualistic abstractions based on eighteenth-century materialism; and it is opposed to all Jacobinistic utopias and innovations. It does not believe in the possibility of "happiness" on earth as conceived by the economistic literature of the XVIIIth century, and it therefore rejects the teleological notion that at some future time the human family will secure a final settlement of all its difficulties.
>
> (Ibid: 174)

From these passages, it is apparent that the main principles of Fascism deny individual rights and freedoms as championed by the thinkers of the Enlightenment. Hence, how can it be claimed that Fascists have an equal, absolute right to communicate? In fact, the international community has endorsed an anti-propaganda position since the ratifying of the *Universal Declaration of Human Rights,* and the United Nations has specifically languaged more than one resolution in the attempt to condemn the communication of propaganda. Among these are the United Nations Educational, Scientific, and Cultural Organization (UNESCO) draft declaration of fundamental principles covering the use of the mass media (January 23, 1974). The excerpts of this report introduced support below certain limits on the absolute

Right to Communicate. For instance, the preamble states the following:

> Recalling that the freedom of expression, information and opinions are fundamental human rights and that the free interchange of accurate, objective and comprehensive information and of opinions, both in the national and in the international spheres, is essential to the cause of peace and the achievement of political, social, cultural, and economic progress.

Also, Article (3) declares: "The right to seek and transmit information should be assured in order to enable the public to ascertain facts and appraise events." Meanwhile, in Article (5) the publication of propaganda is addressed directly: "The dissemination of false reports harmful to friendly relations among nations or inciting to war or to national, racial or religious hatred should be avoided."

Hate Speech versus Free Speech

Can it be claimed that, on the basis of one's absolute right to communicate, one has the right to also voice hate speech? There is a conflict between the values of tolerance and respect for human dignity on the one hand, and the value of free speech and the right to communicate on the other. This conflict is reflected in various contemporary practices that, although seemingly derived from this right, express intolerance for, and cause harm to, certain groups in society.

Salman Rushdie's book *The Satanic Verses* represents one of the greatest problems of absolute free speech. In 1988, Rushdie published a story about a character named "Mahound—which means false prophet . . . a prophet-like figure who is also an unscrupulous, lecherous man (and in no way divine). [Muslims] were appalled by the idea that this figure would have included in the Koran the satanic verses suggested by the devil" (Lee, 1990: 73). Muslims around the world were deeply offended and angered as they felt that their Prophet and their sacred book had been denigrated and interpreted ironically, which was completely unacceptable to them. The Iranian leader at the time issued a *Fatwa* calling for the killing of Rushdie for his "blasphemous deed," displaying a high degree of intolerance. When Rushdie was confronted with these angry reactions to his book, he said, claiming his right to communicate and free speech: "Everything is worth discussing. There are no subjects which are off limits and that includes God, includes prophets" (Rushdie, cited in Lee, 1990: 74).

Opponents of Rushdie's claim for free speech in this case, argue that it is not only Muslims who feel their sacred book or religious beliefs should not be subject to misrepresentation, defamation, or denigration. Lee points out that in Christianity[2] the same idea exists. The Church of England Group, for example, enforces the idea of the "sensitivity" toward sacred books and feelings:

> It is often not so much what the law specifically says as the general underlying attitudes and values which it is held to express that are of importance for social well-being . . . Feelings for the sacred should not be undermined . . . we feel that the public debasement of Christian imagery, besides being deeply offensive to many Christians, may lead to a blindness to the things of the spirit and be seen as a corruption of the mind with regard to what we believe to be the most important features of human life.
>
> (cited in Lee, 1990: 85)

These two opposing positions, which question whether communication is a basic and universal human right or not, are significant to the core of this book. Rushdie's argument, which he believes is backed by the *Universal Declaration of*

Human Rights and other international treaties, is that he holds an absolute freedom to express his opinions and thoughts even though in doing so he might contradict and defame Muslim religion and beliefs. The counter argument claims the opposite, that Rushdie has crossed the line in aggressively portraying sacred texts and revered personalities without regard to others' feelings or thoughts, which could be seen as a kind of hate speech. Which party has the Right to Communicate, Rushdie or those who would draw the line?

Another issue that must be addressed here concerns the vast and diverse quantity of information available via new technologies such as the Internet, and the facility to access and disseminate all kinds of information rapidly, including indecent, offensive, or harmful material such as child pornography. Although access to information on the Internet is currently unrestricted, there are some questions as to whether or not those who disseminate or access offensive material can claim the protection of the law on the basis of their right to communicate. Breckheimer observes, quoting the U.S. Supreme Court[3], that "the content of the Internet is as diverse as human thought" (2002: 1494). This statement points to the complexity of the Internet, where the entire spectrum of humanity is represented, including groups who create Websites[4] to "not only encourage intolerance, but also to promote violence" (Ibid). Can this type of communication be a universal right? Can an absolute Right to Communicate support offensive language, which provokes violence in society?

The Internet, Pornography, and Offensive Signs

Is the right to communication limited to verbal expression, such as speech and written texts, or could it also apply to signs and non-verbal communication that could be claimed as forms of free speech? The case of *Cohen versus the State of*

California, 1971, is an interesting example of the recognition of the individual's right to free speech, even though the particular expression may be offensive to many. In this case, the Supreme Court judged that it was not right for the State of California to convict Cohen because he wore a jacket emblazoned with the phrase "Fuck the Draft," a sign of vulgar discourse, in a corridor of the Los Angeles Courthouse, where many children and women were present. The Supreme Court reasoned:

> How is one to distinguish this form from any other offensive word? Surely the State has no right to cleanse public debate to the point where it is grammatically palatable to the most squeamish among us . . . for, while the particular four-letter word being litigated here is perhaps more distasteful than most others of its genre, it is nevertheless often true that one man's vulgarity is another's lyric.
>
> (cited in Smolla, 1992: 47)

Can pornographers or pornography providers claim legitimacy for their activities based on their right to communicate and free speech? This question targets another controversial area of the application of the universal rights set out in the *Universal Declaration of Human Rights*. Do communication rights apply to this issue? In fact, some consider pornography as one type of communication that obtains its legitimacy from and is protected under the declarations pervasively discussed that advocate an absolute right to communicate. Others take the opposite view. In fact, Lee, taking into account feminist arguments on this matter, contends that pornographic communications discriminate and demonstrate contempt against women. Furthermore, these arguments were heard in North America, and in Canada in particular, where a Royal Commission recommended that materials that abominate and despise women be categorized in the same way as materials depicting violence against women (1990: 36–37). Barron and Dienes argue that one cannot always apply the absolute Right to Communicate and free speech as stated in the *First Amend-*

ment, as there are certain cases where the application could be problematic:

> [I]t is clear that not all acts can generate a persuasive case to First Amendment protection. . . . [A] couple engaged in intercourse on a public street cannot claim first amendment protection as a defense to criminal prosecution, even if in their view they are communicating their belief in a new sexual morality. . . . [W]hat protection does the First Amendment afford to the "topless" dancer who claims a constitutional dimension to her artistic expression.
>
> (1979: 190)

Invasion of Privacy and the Right "Not to Communicate"

Another questionable situation stems from the possible contradiction between the Right to Communicate and the right to privacy. The right to privacy is proclaimed and "stated" in Article (12) of the *Universal Declaration of Human Rights*: "No one shall be subjected to arbitrary interference with his privacy . . . or correspondence." An interesting example that portrays this contradiction in Canada is found in the Report of the House of Commons Standing Committee on Human Rights and the Status of Persons with Disabilities of April 1997. This report discusses privacy as one of the basic human rights, and, at the same time, as a social value that characterizes the Canadian way of life. In the words of the Committee Chair, Sheila Finestone, privacy is a

> core human value that goes to the very heart of preserving human dignity and autonomy; it is a precious resource because once lost, whether intentionally or inadvertently, it can never be recaptured.
>
> (1997: 6)

Thanks to modern technology, the right to privacy is often invaded in certain public places for security purposes, for example, the use of video surveillance in banks, stores, etc. The claim against the use of these monitoring devices is that they violate an individual's right to communicate freely and in privacy as they wish. While it is recognized that everyone has, according to the international declarations, a right to communicate and to privacy, at the same time society has to ensure security for the public at large. So, how can this problem be solved? Following the September 11th, 2001 attacks, and under the state of anti/counter terrorism that preoccupies most of the national and international discourses and spheres today, global communicative patterns have shifted toward highlighting "anti/counter-terrorism" actions, which can be seen as an ongoing elimination of the emphasis of the human right to communicate as a core civil liberty, as stated in Article (19) of the *Universal Declaration of Human Rights* along with the *International Covenant on Civil and Political Rights* (1966), and other international documents. Although the act of terrorism is inherently unacceptable, as the United Nations Secretary General asserted that it is "by its very nature . . . an assault on the fundamental principles of law, order, human rights, and peaceful settlement of disputes upon which the United Nations is established" (Dakroury, 2006: 3). For that, the United Nations has decried the ways in which counter/anti terrorism legislation employed by nations, governments, and states might dangerously serve as "the rationale to crack down on dissident groups and critics of a regime," and moreover, by which this adopted legislation "might infringe on human rights and civil liberties of persons in those states" (Ibid).

Considering the Right to Communicate as absolute and universal raises another important question: if everyone has the right to communicate, does this include the right not to communicate, or the right to privacy? Jean d'Arcy first raised this question in his discussion of Article (19) of *Universal Declaration of Human Rights* and given the "horizontal" flow of information, he questioned the notion of whether "the right to communicate includes the right not to communicate . . . [as] better suited to extricating the discussions on information flow from the deadlock in which they have remained for thirty years," (1982: 7) as outlined in his study included in the MacBride Commission Report. Réné Cassin, head of the French delegate in the United Nations, as Harms and Richstad interpret, says that by combining the statements included in both Articles (19) and (20) that proclaim the right to "seek, receive and impart information and ideas" and the right to a "peaceful assembly and association," is the basis of the communication interaction (Harms & Richstad, 1977: 97). They add that by looking to the second section of Article (20), which states that "no one may be compelled to belong to an association," another question is raised: Is there a Right Not to Communicate, and is this right languaged or not, or acceptable or not? (Ibid). This is an important dimension in realizing how an absolute Right to Communicate can influence the right to privacy, especially in terms of communication rights of cultural minorities. Harms presents, in this context, the Indian philosopher Ghandi's perspective—that some cultures have the right to produce their own values and information from their own culture, and therefore they could proclaim their right "not to communicate" (1982: 5).

Consider the case of child-murderer Clifford Olson, who was sentenced to 25 years in prison without parole. Recently he sought to publish a personal memoir, a request he thought should be granted to him on the basis of his right to freedom of speech and communication. He had in fact applied for, and received, a copyright on a series of 12 videotapes of him discussing his terrible crimes.[5] Can a claim be made for his right to communication?

Olson's case can be discussed in relation to the "clear and present danger" principle, which represents a necessary limitation of the free speech principle under certain conditions. Greenawalt (2002) gives us the historical background of this concept in law, specifically, the *Schenck versus United States* case of 1919. Schenck was convicted of violating the *Espionage Act* of 1917 during World War One. At his trial the presiding judge argued:

> We admit that in many places and in ordinary times the defendants in saying all that was said in the circular would have been within their constitutional rights. But the character of every act depends on the circumstances in which it is done ... the question in every case is whether the words used are used in each circumstance and are of such a nature as to create a clear and present danger that they will bring about the substantive evils that Congress has a right to prevent. It is a question of proximity and degree. When a nation is at war many things that might be said in time of peace is such a hindrance to its effort that their utterance will not be endured so long as men fight and that no Court could regard them as protected by any constitutional right.
>
> (2002: 99)

From the above passage it is clear that "the time" was a stronger reason for Schenck's condemnation than his actual activity, which was circulating anti-war posters to men called for military service. Judge Posner affirms the view that free speech may be limited according to time and circumstance. Hence, he proposes two models of conceiving of free speech: The first he calls "instrumental," by which he means "freedom of speech is to be valued to the extent that it promotes specified goals, such as political stability, economic prosperity and personal happiness." The second is the "moral" approach that embodies the "proper moral conception of persons as rational creatures able to express their ideas and opinions freely and responsibly" (Posner, 2002: 121).

The concept of clear and present danger has been, Greenawalt argues, one of the doctrines used in interpreting the *First Amendment* in recent years. He asks, "To what sorts of communications does the 'clear and present danger' test apply?" (2000: 99). Furthermore, can the Olson diaries represent such a danger?

Media Ownership and Control[6]

The problem of media ownership and control and its impact on the Right to Communicate has long been, and still is, one of the greatest barriers to the enjoyment of this right, and constitutes one of the basic arguments against its universality in practice. This was Jean d'Arcy's argument over two decades ago when complaints and problems arose due to media ownership and monopolies in the communication industry. He says: "Any power, religious, political or private, always knew that control over communication meant control over society. One of the titles of Caesar was 'Pontifex Maximus', the builder of bridges. Control of bridges gives control of roads and thus communications" (d'Arcy, 1977: 49). In another study highlighting the impact of the many levels of "powers" that can dominate and control the right of people to communicate freely, d'Arcy affirms "that he who controls communications effectively controls society" (1969: 2). What would d'Arcy have to say today about conglomerate media ownership as one of the basic impediments to the universal practice of a Right to Communicate?

Basically, the relationship between the field of communications and democracy can be effectively seen through the study of telecommunication (as one of the communication media) in recent years, particularly in the period since the rise of modern technologies. Nevertheless, the field of communication technologies cannot be separated from the socioeconomic realm in which it operates, where democracy flourishes and maintains the development of technology and economics on the one hand, and, on the other, serves the public interest and supports related issues such as the debate over the Right to Communicate, freedom of speech and expression, the right to know, universal access, etc. The basic and most obvious trend in the field of telecommunications in recent years is "convergence" between media and communication corporations. Almost every day there is news of an alliance between giant media concerns, therefore, it is not surprising that the ideal model of the information flow that enables people to enjoy their right to communicate is threatened and in some ways even denied.

In fact, it can be argued that the existence of conglomerates that own different types and genres of media in different fields, through their vertical and horizontal integration, affects the public in three different ways. The first way is that conglomerate ownership limits the enforcement and application of the three forms of freedoms that constitute the Right to Communicate as stated in Article (19) of the *Universal Declaration of Human Rights*. Second, it represents a real threat to the expression of diversity of opinion, especially in the local media where these giant media institutions own cable, newspapers, television stations, etc. Finally, and considering the famous phrase of Marshall McLuhan, "the medium is the message," an important question arises: "Does the one who controls the medium control the content as well?" The answer would have to be yes, one can control the messages by owning different and powerful kinds of media, and this could be seen as a violation of Article (19). It is clear that the problem of conglomerate media ownership is that it threatens the process of sending, receiving, and imparting information at the least, and considerably more aspects of communication at worst (Dakroury, 2005). Jean d'Arcy pinpoints this issue by claiming: "All these are but signs and symptoms veiling a profound revolution, for today we live a revolution of communication . . . the problem of the reception and interpretation of [the] message, is indeed at the heart of our major preoccupation; communication has become our task" (1977: 47).

What would be a good solution in the above-mentioned cases? Should the international declaration of the right to communicate and freedom of speech be applied blindly? Or is the "slippery slope" argument a possible solution? In the pornography debate, if the banning of pornography is the beginning of an unstoppable slide down the slope of increasing censorship, then is the solution to allow pornography as communication, no matter how vile, leaving individuals free to make their own choice to accept or reject it? Or should these materials be banned for the protection of those who might be harmed by them? What other solutions are available? In order to be able to answer these problematic questions, a better understanding of what makes "anything" a "right" is first needed. The following is a discussion and a trial to discover some clues for possible answers.

A Provisional Conceptualization of What Is a "Right"

Why do humans, from childhood to adulthood, claim that they possess certain rights? For instance, why does a young child claim the right to stay up late to watch television? What makes an activist believe that the struggle to publish a book on human rights in a totalitarian regime is worth imprisonment, or even death? What makes such rights that desirable and worth the argument and pain that often accompanies the struggle to gain them? Several important questions arise in the context of this discussion, specifically, of the right to communication and whether communication can be considered a basic human right. What is a right? Where do rights come from? What makes a right desirable? On what basis can it be argued that communication is one of these human rights? In fact, there are various answers to these questions, most of them having to do with issues of morality, ethics, freedom, and equity.

Historically, the idea of a human right is thought to have evolved through three "generations." The first generation covers what are called the negative freedoms, mainly the basic rights of autonomy and security against arbitrary powers in society; England's *Habeas Corpus Act* of 1679 is a good example of negative freedoms (Stoilov, 2001: 88). The second generation includes the economic, social and cultural rights that saw development and recognition particularly in the late nineteenth and early twentieth centuries. People at this time realized the importance of certain rights pertaining to the quality of their lives in developed and modern societies. The third generation, which evolved mainly in the twentieth century, emphasized rights to concepts such as a clean environment, development, and peace, which in earlier centuries were seen as "luxurious" or "undiscovered." From this perspective, certain basic rights had been realized, and it then became possible to focus on other levels of rights. Stoilov argues that after the realization of these third generation rights, and given the continuous development in societies in recent years, one could predict that new rights will eventually be included among existing human rights (2001: 88- 89). In fact, many have argued recently in favour of a fourth generation of human rights that would include, for example, gay and lesbian rights. These, in turn would include their right to marry, which is not covered by Article (16-1) in the *Universal Declaration of Human Rights*:

> Men and women of full age, without any limitation due to race, nationality or religion, have the right to marry and to found a family. They are entitled to equal rights as to marriage, during marriage and at its dissolution.

Defining the concept of a "human right" is not an easy task for several reasons. For example, one must consider the very breadth of rights that are recognized or proclaimed, which varies from fundamental, inalienable rights, to political, civil, cultural, and social rights. Secondly, because human rights are understood within the context of a set of social, political, economic and cultural concepts, they can be regarded, from different perspectives, as absolute and universal on the one hand, or merely socially constructed on the other. In addition, different international, national, regional, and local treatises, conventions, and declarations have proclaimed a number of different human rights. In this book, analysis and discussion are focused on the *Universal Declaration of Human Rights*, the *International Covenant on Civil and Political Rights*, and the *UNESCO Media Declaration*, the international treatises that directly address the Right to Communicate.

Despite the difficulty in defining "human right," a number of scholars have offered various explanations from different perspectives. A good starting point in this context is Baehr's succinct characterization: "Human rights are not absolute" (1999: 1). By this he points, perhaps, to the fact that regardless the number of conferences held or treaties, regulations, declarations, and covenants enacted, since the adoption of the original *Universal Declaration of Human Rights* after the Second World War, one can still claim that these fundamental human rights are neither universally nor identically practised. In every society, these rights are conceived differently according to the norms, values, traditions, culture, of each society. Baehr's conception of human rights, in fact, emphasizes agreement on values: "Human rights are internationally agreed values, standards or rules regulating the conduct of states towards their own citizens and towards non-citizens" (Ibid). Donnelly's similar interpretation adds the dimension of social practices to the recognition of values: "Human rights are not just abstract values, but a set of particular social practices to realise those values" (1999: 79). This interpretation is significant in the context of understanding and explicating the definition of a right and proposes a distinct method for its realization in real life, not only theoretically or in language. It is undeniable that despite their various legal languages, human rights are still violated in many places around the world.

In this context, it is useful to clarify the difference between a "right" and freedom. Aldo Armando Cocca, Ambassador of Argentina and a member of the MacBride Commission during the 1970s, explains that, from a legal perspective, a "right" encompasses a broader scope than freedom: "'Right' has an extremely wide meaning, according to the different legislations and to the way in which it is exercised. It implies abiding by a norm, it is something to be compiled without any qualifications, deviations or hesitations" (1982: 1). From this definition, it can be understood that a "right" implies collectiveness or the exercise of a given freedom in a given society, while "freedom" carries a sense of individuality or the possibility of options or choices beyond collectivity. Viewed in this manner, a right can initially have two main characteristics: the first is the power to exercise a given freedom; the second, the commitment of others not merely to respect this right but to also allow its practice. For Cocca, freedom is "the implementation of universal laws in a given place and time," but, he says, "while 'freedom' implies the power of acting without any interference, 'right' means that plus the obligation of others to allow that action" (1982: 1–2).

Other scholars view human rights from different perspectives, adding other dimensions to the concept. Cranston (1973), for example, offers a classic definition that concentrates on the "universal morality" aspect:

> A human right by definition is a universal moral right, something which all men, everywhere, at all times ought to have, something of which no one may be deprived without a grave affront to justice, something which is owing to every human being simply because he is human.
>
> (cited in Renteln, 1990: 47)

Also Rendel (1997), in his book *Whose Human Rights?*, asserts the importance of morality, but adds religiousness as an important dimension:

> Human rights education has also a moral dimension, as well as a cognitive content. The values of human rights accord with many of the values of most religions, so that many traditional religious beliefs can be linked with at least some modern notions of human rights.
>
> (1997: 179)

Alison Renteln (1990) offers yet another interesting perspective on the meaning of human rights. Focusing on the universality of this concept, he sees its content as based on a combination of four sources: (1) divine authority, (2) natural law, (3) intuition, and (4) ratification of international treaties. Renteln believes that none of these four bases provides full justification for all human rights; moreover, he opposes the natural theory of human rights. "The most misleading source has been natural law because there is an assumption that natural rights, which have become associated with human rights, are self-evident. The rights are held by all individuals simply by virtue of their status as human beings" (1990: 9). Andrew McNitt also discusses the universality perspective in his analysis of human rights. He holds that human rights should be treated as a multidimensional phenomenon, and that approaching the concept in this way will avoid the development of a single, narrow definition (1988: 99).

In light of the above discussion, it can be suggested that the concept "right" exists in "positive law,"[7] that is, in an article, a clause, or a covenant that states a given right—for example, that everyone shall have a certain right to expression, or to movement, and so on. Taking the example of the right to freedom of speech, one finds that there are hundreds of regulations and various legal systems that state this right. From a critical perspective, this law does not discriminate against various persons or groups having the same right; at the same time, however, these laws spell out the violations of the right, such as hate speech or propaganda that might be defended by certain groups as their Right to Communicate (it could be argued that these practices are not typically communication).

Alternatively, rights could be categorized into two main types: moral and legal rights. The first type includes those socially independent rights that are sometimes perceived as natural or human, those claimed "just by virtue of our status as human beings" (Lyons, 1984: 111–112). The second type of rights, legal rights—including both rights that are protected by the law and proclaimed during dealings with the different laws—require a degree of social recognition or enforcement. This is the utilitarianism position that rights are never separate from the social context. In addition, conceptualizing "rights" is not easy given a degree of normative nature, and the fact that even in the same society the standards of morality may vary among different groups. It is instructive to analyze the relationship between the concepts of right and duties that constitute the link between morality and rights. "The existence and irresolvability of diversity and disagreement in ethics," Waldron writes, "pose exactly the same difficulties for talk about moral rights—no more and no less—as they pose for talk about moral duties, rules, principles, and values" (1984: 5).

Perhaps the most comprehensible and plausible standpoint in conceptualizing a "right" on the one hand, and helping to answer the core question of this book on the other, is the significant contribution of the American jurist Wesley Newcomb Hohfeld. Therefore, it may be useful at this point to explain Hohfeld's interpretation of what a right is. If it is unreasonable to assume that someone can claim that s/he holds a right and others, accordingly, are committed not to violate it, can a young child, then for instance, claim a "right" to watch television all day and night?

In his landmark analysis, *Fundamental Legal Conceptions as Applied in Judicial Reasoning* (1919), Hohfeld argues that "rights" imply some corresponding duties on other persons, first not to interfere, and second to assist and cooperate. He says, as Kramer interprets: "Being endowed with a right (also conceived as a 'claim') consists in being normatively protected against someone else's interference or in being entitled to someone else's assistance or remuneration, with regard to a certain action or a certain state of affairs" (1997: 15).

Hohfeld proposes "the table of jural correlatives" to refer to different concepts: Right, Privilege, Power, and Immunity as one axis, and No-Right, Duty, Disability, and Liability as the other. The first correlative relationship is the "Right-Duty" relationship. If someone has a right—"claim-right" in Hohfeld's terminology—this is correlated with a "duty" from others. For example, if X is claiming for his/her right not to be tortured in a prison, it follows that the prison's officials, or Y, have a duty not to torture. Alternatively, if X is sending a letter to the editor of a daily journal, can the claim be made for his/her right to publish it, hence, implying that the editor, or Y, has a duty to publish it? In other words, can communication be one of these strong claim-rights in the Hohfeldian perspective?

> A duty or a legal obligation is that which one ought or ought not to do. "Duty" and "right" are correlative terms. When a right is invaded, a duty is violated.
>
> (Hohfeld, 1919: 13)

Correspondingly, one could see that a violation of a right is an omission of duties, as Kramer suggests: "Anyone who violates a right has thereby failed to live up to the imperatives of a duty. When a person's neglecting of a duty becomes known, it ordinarily or as something more violently coercive" (1997: 16). The position proposed by Hohfeld is understandable here, especially with the acknowledgement of the continuous changes in societies and the time variable. If the "Right-Duty" relationship—or as may be modified in this book to be the "Right-Responsibility"—exists, humans will have considered a balance between their claims for rights and, at the same time, the responsibilities of others not to violate these rights, and probably to morally protect them.

Hohfeld was motivated by his belief that the concept of a "right" has been misinterpreted—by lawyers, advocates of rights, and so on—and has therefore caused many contradictions in understanding. To this end, he proposes a clear distinction between the concepts of "right" and "liberty or privilege:"

> The importance of keeping the conception of a right (or claim) and the conception of a privilege quite distinct from each other seems evident; and; more than that, it is equally clear that there should be a separate term to represent the latter relation. No doubt, . . . it is very common to use the term "right"; indiscriminately, even when the relation designated is really that of "privilege."
>
> (Hohfeld, 1919: 14)

The second correlative is the "Privilege-No right" relationship. This relationship refers to the absence of a "duty." Hohfeld clarifies that "a privilege is the opposite of a duty, and the correlative of a 'no-right'" (Ibid). When someone has a privilege to do something, this means that s/he is free from a duty to avoid it. At the same time, if privilege to refrain from doing something is freedom from a duty to undertake this action (Kramer, 1997: 16–17).

To distinguish between these two concepts, right and privilege, let us consider two cases. First, if X has a privilege to worship what s/he believes in, this means that Y is under "no duty" toward X in exercising his/her privilege or freedom and has no obligation to help X in completing this action. Differently, if X holds a claim-right for healthcare, for example, Y, the medical system in this case, is obligated to assist and provide X with healthcare services. A timely question here can be: What about communication? Under which relationship can we classify its practice, the liberty or the claim-right?

The third relationship is the "Power-Liability" correlative. Power is a cooperative control that may be imposed on others. If X possesses a power, s/he would possibly change or alter legal relations, thus others would be responsible to let X practice his/her power. Hohfeld clarifies that liability is not just a legal duty; it is a "responsibility":

> The words "debt" and "liability" are not synonymous, and they are not commonly so understood. As applied to the pecuniary relations of the parties, liability is a term of broader significance than debt . . . liability is responsibility.
>
> (Hohfeld, 1919: 27)

Central to the core question of this book, this point is crucial and may lead to insightful answers. It clarifies that "liberty" is a sole or individual practice of X doing something, while both "claim-right" and "power" require a "collective" performance by others, and accordingly, X can do what s/he wants. In this case, education, for example, can be considered a "right," even though X cannot claim for his right to education unless others do not interfere with his/her choice to receive education, help him/her to practice this right, and express responsibilities towards him/her. Once again, is this case applicable to communication practices?

"Immunity-Disability" relationship is the fourth and final correlative in the Hohfeldian connection, where he argues that immunity occurs with the existence of changes in power relations and the freedom from legal power or control undertaken by others. For example, if X holds immunity against doing something, Y will be considered under a status of disability to control this freedom. Considering the case of taxes, if person X, under specific conditions or for specific reasons, can obtain an exemption or immunity to pay taxes, then Y, federal taxes officials in this case, will be unable to enact tax laws against X. Is there any possibility for communication to represent such a case?

Although Hohfeld's correlative relationships represent a powerful position on human rights, a minor objection of the "claim-right" versus "duty" relationship is introduced here. It is argued that a "duty" is sometimes expected even when a "right" is not claimed. Consider the duties toward children or disabled people who cannot claim several of their rights. Interestingly enough, some advocates for the rights of animals take the same standpoint. To explain further, there are two different theories about whether children or animals possess "rights" even though they cannot claim them. First, the "Interest Theory" confirms that: "Necessary but insufficient for the actual holding of a right by X is that the right, when actual, protects one or more of X's interests." Second, the "Will Theory" proposes that: "The mere fact that X is competent and authorized to demand or waive the enforcement of a right will be neither sufficient nor necessary for X's holding of that right" (Kramer, 2001: 28).

Based on this argument, it is clear that, according to the "Will Theory," children, handicapped, incapable humans, and even animals do not possess any rights, as they are incapable of making decisions or expressing their preferences and wishes. In contrast, the "Interest Theory" considers them, Kramer explains, as "rights-holders" that preserve their well-being and are superior than their exercise of their freedom of choice: "[The Interest theory's main focus is] on the preservation of well-being rather than on the exercise of choice enables it to leave open the possibility of ascribing legal rights to animals and dead people and mentally incapacitated people . . . In this respect, the Interest Theory is superior to the Will Theory" (2001: 30).

Accordingly, it is proposed here that one of the critical parameters in conceptualizing an action, whether to be a "right" or not, is the reciprocal relationship between an "interest" and a "duty" or "responsibility." The child can claim for his or her interest to watch television all day and night, meanwhile parents, both legally and morally, have a duty to not to let the child watch television endlessly. Legally, a parent is responsible for protecting and ensuring the mental and physical safety of her daughter or son and if she violates her daughter or son's rights to be fed, for instance, she will be committed guilty by authorities. As well, she is morally responsible for keeping her daughter or son safe and healthy. Therefore, the mother's duty is superior on her daughter or son's interest in watching television—putting it in another way, the child's interest in fact what the parent performs rather than the child considers as best for him or herself.

Contrary to the previously mentioned perspective, Mackie in his *Can There be a Right-Based Moral Theory?*, argues that "right" is more fundamental than duty:

> Rights have obvious advantages over duties as the basis and ground of morality. Rights are something that we may well want to have; duties are irksome. We may be glad that duties are imposed on others, but only (unless we are thoroughly bloody-minded) for the sake of the freedom, protection, or other advantages that other people's duties secure for us and our friends, the point of there being duties must lie elsewhere. Duty for duty's sake is absurd, but rights for their own sake are not.
>
> (1984: 171)

It is worthy here, in context of Mackie's conceptualization, to emphasize the significance of the "interest" or the "want" variable in determining whether an action can be considered a "right" or not. For Mackie, possessing a right is more important than being obliged by a duty or responsibility. Saying that, Mackie takes an "egotistic" position, especially when considering the social context and the more balanced Hohfeldian position. According to Mackie's statement, a daughter or a son can claim a right to watch television all day and night, while a mother's duty and responsibility for her child's health and performance at school comes in a second level of importance. What if the persistent question of this book arises here again? Is it possible to consider the interest of X to publish pornographic materials, claiming a right to communication and expecting others to have a "duty" to let him/her publish these materials? What can possibly be the appropriate position: Mackie's or Hohfeld's? Is there a third position?

In this respect, the review the pertinent literature on this subject confirms that the origins of the concept "right," especially with regard to the core theme of this book— communication— are extremely ambiguous and uncertain.

> My right to life is not a right against anyone. It is my right and by virtue of it, it is normally permissible for me to sustain my life in the face of obstacles. It does give rise to rights against others in the sense that others have or may come to have duties to refrain from killing me, but it is essentially a right of mine, not an infinite list of claims, hypothetical and actual, against an infinite number of actual, potential, and as yet nonexistent human beings . . . Similarly, the right of the tennis club member to play on the club courts is a right to play, not a right against some vague group of potential or possible obstructers.
>
> (cited in Feinberg, 1979: 90)

Inconceivably, McCloskey suggests that the claims of X for a certain right and considers his/her possession of this right and is not in opposition to Y, or anyone else for that matter. Theoretically, X may claim a right without being against Y, or anyone, such as the case of rights to education, health, marriage, or having a family. Nonetheless, putting the "right" in this oppositional relationship is inappropriate. A better understanding can be derived from Hohfeld's correlative relationships, i.e., X can claim for his/her right to life, and accordingly Y is endowed by a duty to respect X's claim, not to interfere, to cooperate and support his/her practice of that right. Also, McCloskey's argument that a claim for a right is similar to playing tennis in a club is, again, a sort of undermining of the importance of the "right" concept. Basically, playing tennis in a club requires a membership and therefore is not a right for everyone. Instead, McCloskey's can be considered more of a privilege according to Hohfeld's theory. If X has a privilege to play tennis in a club, Y is not necessarily to be under a duty to assist him to play.

Still, Joseph Raz provides another comprehensible perspective on the nature and applicability of the concept of a "right." He argues that a right may exist and claim its "collectiveness" under three main conditions: a right should be in the interest of "humanism"; a right should be collective, shared and serve a "public good" for all members of the group; and finally, the interest of a single member of a group justifies the other members being bound by duty to act in that interest, which explains why "though the existence of the right does not depend on the size of the group, its weight or strength does" (1984: 194).

Drawing from the foregoing overview of scholarly conceptualization of rights, the position adopted here is that both a claim to a right, and a duty, obligation or responsibility toward it, could be derived from many different sources. For example, the natural rights school of thought believes in the natural origin of fundamental rights and freedoms: men are born by nature free. Similarly, there are other possible origins of right and duty, such as God-given or divine, utility, morality, positive laws, and conscience. As X can claim that God is creator, God also gave him/her the right to free choices in life and no one can take this right away. Therefore, s/he can claim free movement because the land is God's creation as well as claim equality between him/herself and others as God creates all of humans equals. Furthermore, a claim to one right may be derived from another right, and it may also contain other sub-rights, as Mackie suggests: "Rights can be derived from other rights in fairly obvious logical ways" (1984: 170).

To claim the right to publish a book, for example, one can argue it is based on a right to impart and exchange information with other readers. At the same time, the right to publish a book includes other sub-rights, such as the right to freedom of expression. The reasons underlying an obligation toward others may be also one's conscience, or fear of God, or respect for the law, or fear of the punishment that may result from violation of the law, and so on. The activist who claims the right to publish a book on human rights builds his/her claim on conscience—his/her belief that it is important to help other violated peoples; or on his/her entitlement to publish as the practice of his right to freedom of expression. Wasserstrom says: "To have a right to anything is, in short, to have a very strong moral or legal claim upon it. It is the strongest kind of claim" (1979: 48).

Fundamentally, a right may exist even though there is a lack of liberties. Acknowledging, for instance, a right of a prisoner not to be tortured or humiliated does not deny the fact that s/he cannot practice other liberties, or sometimes face some constraints to these liberties: such as the liberty of movement. The main point to emphasize here is that a right not to be tortured does not weight in importance, at least practically, a right such as communication, unless every prisoner could claim for his/her right to have a telephone in his/her prison cell, just like his claim not to be tortured while s/he is in prison!

Furthermore, a right can exist also in different spheres or contexts, such as religious, legal, social, moral or political spheres. The bottom line of a claim for these rights is, as Shapiro suggests, "via mutual consent" (1986: 61) among individuals in a given society. In other words, a consensus among individuals on a right means that they are "accepting," "respecting," and consequently, and more importantly, "obliged" to protect it from violations. For example, when a right to health care captures a wide-range consensus in a society, it is undeniable that everyone, including the state, is obliged to accept, respect, and protect this right from violation as well as to assist practicing it.

To come to the point, this book proposes a provisional conceptualization of a right and whether communication can be considered as one of these rights or not. Through adopting a Hohfeldian position, it may become clear that the reciprocal relationship between the right and the individual's duty to uphold the same right for others is important, the same as the right itself is. One could consider the following understanding of what responsibility is:

> A man is responsible for his actions because in acting he acts in his own, unique situation, into which he may bring his fellows' interests, or he may not. He may withdraw from his place in society if he so desires, and thus his responsibility for what he does in society is a relation between his own situation and those of others who are affected by his actions.
>
> (Roberts, 1965: 309)

In view of that, the following is an effort to find out, through a historical exploration of relevant texts, whether or not one can claim that all human beings, without any distinction, possess a right to practice communication, i.e., communication can be considered as one of the basic human rights or not. The next step is an investigation of the various and different philosophical and intellectuals' literature and positions, to figure out how they understand communication and whether they believe or not that it can be one of the basic human rights. More importantly, what do these philosophers and thinkers support: an absolute right to communicate, as "stated" and proclaimed in the various declarations, whatever the results are; a restriction of some of these rights for "good" reasons; or a different offered comprehensive and less problematic situation?

Notes

1. I have analyzed this controversy from a human right perspective in the 2nd Canadian conference of the Association of Muslim Social Scientists (AMSS)—Canada. *Islam: Tradition and Modernity*. Organized by The Association of Muslim Social Scientists (AMSS)-Canada and The Department of Near and Middle Eastern Civilizations, University of Toronto, Canada.

2. Simon Lee refers to the English Commission for Racial Equality and Interfaith in his discussion of this particular story, especially in regard to the history of blasphemy in the English Law (1990: 75–93).

3. Reno v. ACLU, 521 U.S. 844, 870 (1997).

4. Breckheimer gives many examples of Websites that encourage "hate speech," for example, the anti-Women, anti-White, anti-Gay sites that not only disseminate words or actions but also provide interactive hate games and hate music (2002: 1494–1495). It is worth noting here that as a result of the increase in amount and types of hate speech around the world, many countries, such as Germany, have undertaken legal procedures to regulate the use of communication channels for hate speech. Canada is among the countries that have taken some minor measures to restrict hate speech under special conditions. In Canada, for example, section (2) of the *Canadian Charter of Rights and Freedoms* defines the right to free speech, but with what Breckheimer (2002) calls a "spirit of balance" between "individuals' free speech rights" and "societal equality interests" (1514). The Canadian Supreme Court (The Queen v. Keegstra, 1990, S.C.R. 697, 743) however, states that in the "uniquely Canadian vision of a free and democratic society . . . the suppression of hate propaganda is incompatible with the guarantee of free expression" (Ibid).

5. For the full story, see: http://www.crimelibrary.com/serial_killers/predators/olson/20.html?sect=2.

6. An example of recent complaints regarding the practice of some giant conglomerate media and their interference in the editorial policy of their newspapers chains, see The Canadian Journalists for Free Expression (CJFE) and the case of *CanWest Global* (http://www.cjfe.org/specials/canwest/canwintro.html). See also Dakroury, 2005.

7. There are two categories of rights: positive or legal rights and negative rights. Positive rights are enforced and maintained by different laws or regulations and require assistance from others. Negative rights, referring to the corresponding entailment of other persons for non-interference, may involve moral, natural, or human rights. Raymond Geuss argues that the first category includes objective rights; the second, subjective. The difference between these two categories, in his opinion, is that one could claim an objective right with the expectation that other members of the society would respect and not violate it, and that a power exists in the society to guarantee and protect it. This is not the case with a subjective right (which might be shared with animals for instance) (2001: 133–135).

Chapter 4

Philosophical Foundation of Communication as a "Human Right"

> If we think to regulate printing, thereby to rectify manners, we must regulate all recreations and pastimes, all that is delightful to man. No music must be heard, no song be set or sung, but what is grave and Doric . . . And who shall silence all the airs and madrigals that whisper softness in chambers? . . . twenty licensors?
>
> *(Milton, 1644: 23–24)*

> Freedom being the foundation of all the rest; as he that, in the state of society, would take away the freedom belonging to those of that society or commonwealth, must be supposed to design to take away from them everything else.
>
> *(Locke, 1690: 463)*

> To have a right, then, is, I conceive, to have something which society ought to defend me in the possession of. If the objector goes on to ask why it ought, I can give him no other reason than general utility.
>
> *(Mill, 1861: 326)*

The discussion in this chapter argues that the concept of a possible Right to Communicate is rooted in the ideas of certain thinkers of the so-called *Age of Reason* beginning in the seventeenth century. Through an analysis of the ideas of John Milton, John Locke, Voltaire, Montesquieu, Jeremy Bentham, and John Stuart Mill, I shall explore the development of the conception of the Right to Communicate.

John Milton (1608–1674): Early Uni-Dimensional Right

Before beginning any discussion of the core thinkers of the Enlightenment, it is helpful to look at the work of the seventeenth century English writer and poet John Milton (1608–1674). In this chapter he is placed among those earlier thinkers who claimed, at least, a limited or a one-dimensional right to communicate. In his focus on pre-publication censorship as a violation of the right to communicate, he does not claim that this right is universal or open and "available for all." In examining his philosophy, two questions pertinent to this book come to mind: 1) Is freedom of the press or authorship the only kind of communication that could be assumed to be a right? 2) Is it only literate or educated people who can claim the right to communicate? If the answer to the second question is "yes," the question must then be asked: was Milton against the "universality" of this right?

Milton was the most prominent thinker of his time to advocate freedom of the press and speak out against pre-publication censorship. Palumbo, in his exploration of the history of human rights, describes how Milton fought during the 1640s for liberty of the press and an end to government control over political and religious writings. For Milton, Palumbo says, "the right freely to seek the truth was absolutely fundamental to Christianity and human dignity, and it was totally mistaken to try to define it by law" (1982: 29).

Milton, in his landmark *Areopagitica*, published in 1644, explicitly conjoins communication and freedom of expression as an important right, for example, in his connotation of the birth of ideas as the birth of a human being: "Till then books were ever freely admitted into the world as any other birth; the issue of the brain was no more stifled than the issue of the womb" (1644: 13). In his speech addressed to the British Parliament, Milton defends several types of freedoms and liberties that combine a possible right to communicate, he says:

> If it be desired to know the immediate cause of all this free writing and free speaking . . . it is liberty, Lords and Commons . . . liberty which is the nurse of all great wits; this is that which hath rarefied and enlightened our spirits like the influence of heaven . . . give me the liberty to know, to utter, and to argue freely according to conscience, above all liberties.
>
> (Milton, 1644: 48–49)

Subsequently, he decries the "violent," "physical" hands of the licensor, pointing out that the licensor violates the author's human existence by attempting to constrain his mind through censoring the "body" of the printed text—the representation of his thought. Sherman explains:

> The mind thinks itself into print, where its re-embodiment is the printed text. Physicality is conferred on agencies that would—unnaturally—turn the author back into a "writer," insisting upon his creating a manuscript that they can "blot and alter," disrupting the mind/press relationship.
>
> (1993: 325)

What Milton claims here is one form of the right to communicate freely without frontiers, especially in his notion of the freedom to send ideas or messages from the mind through the media of the press and books—the only media of communication that existed during his time, refuting accusations that Milton only defended "printed" media. The licensor as gatekeeper represented for Milton the frontier that stands between the human mind and the books or press as embodiments of the messages. That is why, as Sherman writes, "Milton demands that even though controversial books may be dangerous to the learned, 'those books must be permitted untouched by the licensor'" (Ibid: 326). A closer look at two key passages in Milton's *Areopagitica* reveals how he conceives communication as a basic, even sacred, right:

> I deny not, . . . to have a vigilant eye how books demean themselves, as well as men; and thereafter to confine, imprison, and do sharpest justice on them as malefactors; for books are not absolutely dead things, but do contain a progeny of life in them to be as active as that soul was whose progeny they are; nay, they do preserve as in a vial the purest efficacy and extraction of that living intellect that bred them I know they are lively, and vigorously productive as those fabulous dragon's teeth; . . . And yet . . . unless wariness be used, as good almost kill a man as kill a good book: who kills a man kills a reasonable creature, God's image; but he who destroys a good book, kills reason itself, kills the image of God, as it were, in the eye.
>
> (Milton, 1644: 5–6)

According to Milton, not only the "living intellect," but also all other manifestations of human creativity would be regulated by pre-publication censorship. Here he is ironically questioning how a licensor can mute communication by his actions, through including different types of communication media, in addition to the books, such as music, dancing, and even windows and balconies:

> If we think to regulate printing, thereby to rectify manners, we must regulate all recreations and

> pastimes, all that is delightful to man. No music must be heard, no song be set or sung, but what is grave and Doric. There must be licensing dancers, that no gesture, motion, or deportment be taught our youth . . . And who shall silence all the airs and madrigals that whisper softness in chambers? The windows also, and the balconies, must be thought on; there are shrewd books, with dangerous frontispieces, set to sale: who shall prohibit them shall twenty licensors?
>
> (Ibid: 23–24)

It is clear from these brief extracts that Milton equates the book with the highest function of the human mind, the faculty of reason; hence censorship, the physical control of the book, is equivalent in his view to violating the mind – a violation of the human right to freely exercise the God-given power of reason. It could therefore be argued that freedom of communication in the way Milton describes—the conception of communication as freedom of thought, freedom to disseminate and have access to information and ideas, and freedom from the discrimination of censorship—were understood by him as an essential human right.

The question of universality must still be addressed in Milton's works. Willmoor Kendall makes a strong case that Milton did not believe in a universal or absolute right to communicate for all human beings. In his *How to Read Milton's Areopagitica*, Kendall clearly argues, through a close reading of the *Areopagitica*, that although Milton supports freedom of thought and expression and rejects licensing, he does not reject censorship "after" books are published.

More important proof of Milton's non-universalistic stance on the right to communicate in the *Areopagitica*, Kendall argues, is his differentiation between two main categories of humans: the literate, learned and educated man, like himself, who seeks "truth," and the ordinary person who is concerned only with day-to-day affairs and problems. Kendall argues that we can understand Milton's true attitude by reading his texts more closely and between the lines. He takes Milton's famous phrase, "Give me the liberty to know, to utter, and to argue freely, according to conscience, above all liberties," and gives us the following interpretation: "Give me [that is, us] the liberty [what I want for myself, what I am prepared to do battle for, is my liberty and that of other learned men] to know, to utter, and to argue freely, according to conscience" (1960: 447). Milton, Kendall explains, differentiates between individuals according to an important communicative criterion, that is, the mastery of rhetoric or public speaking. Moreover, Milton refers in many places in *Aeropagitica* to "we" and Englishmen, and frequently to "England." Kendall suggests that Milton did not differentiate only between literate men and others within England, but considered the right to communicate to be exclusive to "literate English men."[1]

Furthermore, Milton is raising the "book-burning principle," that also distinguishes between a "good book" and a "bad book." A good book for him is one that teaches what is good, truthful, moral, and right, while a bad book teaches the opposite, that which is bad, false, immoral, and wrong. The point is that it is the duty of society to realize this difference and to act towards eliminating these "bad books."

With Kendall's arguments above, and a careful reading of Milton's own words, we can find his argument is certainly more convincing and comprehensible. He says hereunder that people should allow any kind of books, "bad" and "good," in society, just like allowing good and bad meat in the market. A "True Christian" would be able then to choose and judge what is appropriate from these ideas and thoughts and what is not:

> To the pure all things are pure; not only meats and drinks, but all kind of knowledge whether of good and evil; the knowledge cannot defile, nor consequently the books if the will and conscience be not defiled. For books are as meats and viands are; some of good, some of evil substance. . . . Whole-

> some meats to a vitiated stomach differ little or nothing from unwholesome; and best books to a naughty mind are not unappliable to occasions of evil. Bad meats will scarce breed good nourishment in the healthiest concoction; but herein the difference is of bad books, that they to a discreet and judicious reader serve in many respects to discover, to confute, to forewarn, and to illustrate.
>
> (Milton, 1644: 16)

It is clear from this passage that he is claiming that all books have to be published "uncensored," but once it is determined they are "bad," they should be removed, burnt, or confined. Moreover, while he asserts the importance of having both bad and good books in order to have choices, then confining bad books, he is also demanding not to kill good books.

As for Kendall's argument concerning Milton's distinction between literate and ordinary men, it could be said first that he is mainly concerned with the idea of truth, just like any philosopher who seeks to achieve a high degree of morality in human action. This knowledge for him is therefore not available for all ordinary people, but only for those who appreciate and esteem wisdom. Moreover, he did not mention in his text that if the works of "literate men" proved to be "false" or "bad," they should not be confined or burned. Secondly, Kendall's argument can be refuted logically by noting that Milton was simply addressing the English Parliament, hence, it is comprehensible to include in many places of his *Areopagitica* the notion of "English men." An assertion on these two points is hereunder, where he logically justifies his position against censorship of any kind, just like life that embodies evil and good, knowledge must provide humans by both kinds "good" and "bad:"

> Good and evil we know in the field of this world grow up together almost inseparably; and the knowledge of good is so involved and interwoven

> with the knowledge of evil, and in so many cunning resemblances hardly to be discerned . . . It was from out the rind of one apple tasted, that the knowledge of good and evil, as two twins cleaving together, leaped forth into the world. And perhaps this is that doom which Adam fell into of knowing good and evil, that is to say of knowing good by evil.
>
> (Milton, 1644: 17–18)

A final note concerning Milton's contribution to the idea of communication as a human right is his early one-dimensional perspective of communication. Although, he defended freedom of thought, speech, press, and authorship, he regarded this right universal only "before publishing" one's ideas and opinions on one phase, rather, on the post-publication phase. In other words, he allows communication to be censored, confined, or even burnt under specific conditions:

> As for regulating the press, let no man think to have the honor of advising ye better than yourselves have done in that order published next before this, that no book be printed, unless the printer's and the author's name, or at least the printer's, be registered. Those which otherwise come forth, if they be found mischievous and libellous, the fire and the executioner will be the timeliest and the most effectual remedy that man's prevention can use.
>
> (Ibid: 55)

He illustrates the same idea of uni-dimensional right to communicate, setting up his appropriate punishment for "bad" books, he says:

> Had any one written and divulged erroneous things and scandalous to honest life, misusing and

forfeiting the esteem had of his reason among men, if after conviction this only censure were adjudged him, that he should never henceforth write but what were first examined by an appointed officer, whose hand should be annexed to pass his credit for him that now might be safely read, it could be apprehended less than a disgraceful punishment.

(Ibid: 32)

As seen, Milton's dedication to a "spirit of free inquiry" led him to postulate a limited or a uni-dimensional right to communicate. The following is a discussion on the philosophy of John Locke and what can he offer to the thought of communication as a human right.

John Locke (1632–1704): Absolute Individual Freedom

A key thinker, whose philosophy and ideas contained the seeds that flourished as the basic ideas of human rights in general, and the right to communicate in particular, was the English philosopher John Locke (1632–1704). Peter Schouls' *Reasoned Freedom: John Locke and the Enlightenment* explores the work of Locke, particularly his ideas of freedom, progress, rationality, and mastery, which represent core concepts in Enlightenment thought. Schouls, while acknowledging that Locke was indebted to the French philosopher René Déscartes, one of the "Enlightenment's greatest forefathers," argues that Locke was "the Enlightenment's greatest progenitor" (1992: 3). For instance, Voltaire, one of this period's great writers, wrote in his *Lettres sur les Anglais,* acknowledging Locke and his contribution: "Never has there existed perhaps an intelligence so wise, so methodical, so logical . . . Many philosophers have written romances about the soul of man. Locke appeared quite modestly and wrote its history. He has been the greatest influence since Plato" (cited in Nicolson, 1960: 274).

Locke was influenced by many different streams of thought, all of which affected his philosophy and ideas. Among these were his religious faith and loyalty to Christianity, the political movement that concentrated on tolerance, sovereignty, and political power, and the impact of the modern liberal that concentrated on the rights and freedoms of thought, expression, speech and conscience (Creppell, 1996: 232–233). His philosophy is mainly rooted in the area where religion and morality intersect. His understanding of morality is grounded firmly in the Bible, and he was skeptical about different opinions that could distort the practice of moral principles between humans. Creppell adds that the idea of liberalism arose initially as a way to resolve and overcome the religious intolerance and the resulting violence and oppression that were widespread during Locke's time (Ibid: 200–201).

Many human rights theorists and thinkers believe that Locke's work constitutes the foundation of the modern conception of human rights. Historically, the idea of human rights, many scholars argue, is rooted in the Lockean principles of natural law and private property. For example, Jack Donnelly, one of the prominent human rights theorists, confidently maintains that "John Locke's *Second Treatise on Government* . . . presented the first fully developed natural rights theory fundamentally consistent with later human rights ideas" (1999: 82).[2] These principles permeate Locke's work:

> All men may be restrained from invading others rights, and from doing hurt to one another, and the law of nature be observed, . . . the law of nature is . . . put into every man's hands, whereby everyone has a right to punish the transgressors of that law to such a degree as may hinder its violation.
>
> (Locke, 1690*b*: 458)

Central to his philosophy is the concept of "freedom," the main focus of any discussion of human rights is that every human being is free to act reasonably according to his own will and belief. Included here is an adept example Locke's perception of the concept where he firmly emphasizes that if we give away our freedom as human beings, then we should be prepared to give anything else: "Freedom being the foundation of all the rest; as he that, in the state of society, would take away the freedom belonging to those of that society or commonwealth, must be supposed to design to take away from them everything else" (Ibid: 463). Moreover, Locke applied this concept to many aspects of human life in his concern with human understanding and how individuals exercise "freedom of the will" in their lives. Concerning the principles of freedom and equality, Locke writes: "Men being, as has been said, by nature, all free, equal, and independent, no one can be put out of this estate, and subjected to the political power of another, without his own consent" (Locke, 1690b: 470).

One should note the occurrence of the Lockean exact words of "by nature," "free," and "equal" in the American and French *Declarations*, followed by *the Universal Declaration of Human Rights* in 1948, discussed in Chapter 2, as proof of the impact of his standpoint on the idea of human rights in general and the Right to Communicate in particular. In his *Of the Conduct of the Understanding* essay (paragraph 12), for example, Locke asserts the importance of the "freedom of the understanding" for all people as "free humans" and "rational creatures," and rejects the imposition of ideas that are not our own which constitute constraints on freedom of thought, speech, and expression:

> It is conceit, fancy, extravagance, anything rather than understanding, if it [freedom] must be under the constraint of receiving and holding opinions by the authority of anything but their own, . . . This was rightly called imposition, and is of all other the worst and most dangerous sort of it.
>
> (cited in Schouls, 1992: 7)

A second concept, which Locke emphasizes as one of the core human goals, is the idea of the personal "mastery" of one's own mind, an idea that is reflected in the terminology of self-determination, personal will, and rationality that is employed by many of the Enlightenment philosophers. In many places in his writings, Locke asserts his belief in the power of human rationality and the individual's freedom to use and express that rationality without constraint by authoritative powers such as the church and the state. For Locke, freedom, rationality, liberty, and mastery could not be achieved without a given medium of communication, that is, the holding and exchanging of ideas and opinions. Hence, human liberty begins with mental freedom and the Right to Communicate, as clarified in his *Essay Concerning Human Understanding:*

> The other fountain from which experience furnisheth the understanding with ideas, is the perception of the operations of our own minds within us, as it is employed about the ideas it has got; which operations when the soul comes to reflect on and consider, do furnish the understanding with another sets of ideas, which could not be had from things without; and such are perception, thinking, doubting, believing, reasoning, knowing, willing, and all the different actings of our own minds.
>
> (Locke, 1690a: 355)

On the same point, Locke conceives knowledge as attainable by humans through the exercise of the "natural faculties" of the mind, as he pinpoints in his one of his other essays, *Essay on the Laws of Nature* (1663):

> Careful reflection, thought, and attention by the mind is needed, in order that by argument and reasoning one may find a way from perceptible and obvious things into their hidden nature. . . . [H]uman beings besides are possessed of arms

and hands with which they can dig these out, [gold and silver] and of reason which invents machines.

(cited in Kramer, 1997: 110)

A closer investigation of Locke's work is needed to reveal his conception of communication and his argument for communication as a basic human right. First, it is necessary to highlight the significance of human communication, that is, the sharing of ideas between people, according to Locke's philosophy. At the same time, communication for Locke also describes the exchange of ideas using different media:

> The ideas we get by more than one sense are of space or extension, figure, rest and motion; for these make perceivable impressions, both on the eyes and touch: and we can receive and convey into our minds the ideas of the extension, figure, motion, and rest of bodies, both by seeing and feeling.
>
> (Locke, 1690a: 363)

Does Locke propose freedom of speech? It is clear from his arguments for individual liberty and freedom of thought that he does; he would not separate freedom of thought from freedom of expression or sharing of thought, that is, communication; and that he would include both in the idea of the Right to Communicate. Locke defended individual liberty and freedom in many ways. When considering the production of ideas, signs, and language, in whatever form, as property, anyone who tries to control or eliminate this property can be considered as violating someone's rights. Locke realized that individuals, and individuals alone, can preserve and maintain their own freedoms and rights: "Knowledge can serve as the basis of liberation: individuals see things as they are for themselves, not as they are painted by church, Crown, or custom" (Peters, 1999: 82). In another part of his *Essay Concerning Human Understanding* (1690a), Locke clearly defends freedom of expression and the right to communicate. As Peters explains, quoting Locke, "Language is 'the great instrument, and common Tye of society' that God gave to humans, so they could be sociable creatures" (Ibid: 83). Considering Locke's conception of freedom of speech and the right to communicate as discussed above, it is likely that he was also defending the free exchange of ideas using any medium in the society. In his words, "Language makes the inner life of ideas . . . publicly accessible."[3]

Collectively, one could argue that Locke's true belief in human mastery, rationality, and free will led him to advocate an absolute and universal Right to Communicate. He asserts that "general and universal belong not to the real existence of things; but are the inventions and creatures of the understanding, made by it, for its own use, and concern only signs, whether words or ideas" (Locke, 1690a: 410).

Baron de Montesquieu (1689–1755): Legal Realization of Liberties

Among the contributors to the realization of a possible right to communicate is the political thinker Charles de Secondat, Baron de Montesquieu (1689–1755). His philosophy is mainly embodied in his landmark *Esprit des Lois*—or *The Spirit of Laws*. Initially, Montesquieu differentiates between two kinds of liberties: political liberty and philosophical liberty. First, political liberty, for him, requires a democratic legislature and a judiciary that would uphold "positive laws" guaranteeing liberty for all citizens equally and without distinction. The starting point for him is the human will as being conjoined with reason to form a state of law that regulates freedom:

> In What Liberty Consists. It is true that in democracies the people seem to act as they please; but political liberty does not consist in an unlimited freedom . . . liberty can consist only in the power of doing what we ought to will, and in not being constrained to do what we ought not to will. . . . *Liberty is a right of doing whatever the laws permit*, and if a citizen could do what they forbid he would be no longer possessed of liberty.
>
> (Montesquieu, 1748: 150, *emphasis added*)

We can infer from Montesquieu's words that he rejected absolute political freedom or liberty. In other words, it is necessary in his vision to regulate this kind of liberty to ensure that all citizens enjoy the same freedom, not only those with power. This is the main idea of a positive law. At the same time, Montesquieu did not believe that it should be left to the judiciary alone to oversee human liberty. He insists on communication between the two most important powers in society, the "legislative" and the "executive," to ensure that liberty is protected. Montesquieu proposes a social structure that would include democratically elected representatives of the people to monitor the legislative and executive powers. He cautions, however, in such a state it is essential that the practice of liberty be balanced by respect for the law. He adds that applying an extreme form of equality could be as dangerous as not applying it at all, "Democracy has, therefore, two excesses to avoid: the spirit of inequality, which leads to aristocracy or monarchy, and the spirit of extreme equality, which leads to despotic power, as the latter is completed by conquest" (Ibid: 110).

Philosophical liberty is the second kind of liberty for Montesquieu, which may be representing a possible Right to Communicate. Through using this kind of liberty, according to Montesquieu, people express their own opinions and thoughts freely, but at the same time "agreeably" to the social system. He explains: "Philosophical liberty consists in the free exercise of the will; or at least, if we must speak agreeably to all system, in an opinion that we have the free exercise of our will" (Ibid: 183).

In this context, Montesquieu, defending the Right to Communicate, criticized arbitrary authorities that punish people because they exercise their freedom of speech, in other words, he was supporting an absolute right to communicate "philosophical" ideas and not "political" ones. At the same time, he believes that freedom of speech should not include such a lack of consideration for society and its members:

> Nothing renders the crime of high treason more arbitrary than declaring people guilty of it for indiscreet speeches. Speech is so subject to interpretation; there is so great difference between indiscretion and malice; and frequently so little of the latter in the freedom of expression.
>
> (Ibid: 193)

Montesquieu clarifies also that the acceptance of the satirical and ironic methods of writings and criticism is a key determinant of a government's degree of democracy and freedom. As in monarchies, these methods of writings—though according to Montesquieu as ways of expressing own wills—are absolutely forbidden and are punishable by immediate death:

> Satirical writings are hardly known in despotic governments, where dejection of mind on the one hand, and ignorance on the other, afford neither abilities nor will to write. [While] in democracies they are not hindered, for the very same reason which causes them to be prohibited in monarchies; being generally levelled against men of power and authority.
>
> (Ibid: 195)

Montesquieu is providing a reason for why people, when expressing their opinions freely, should remain within the social system's moral boundaries. For him, the human being is a social creature that has to respect social and moral rules in order to gain the acceptance of the public: "Man, a sociable animal, is formed to please in society; and a person that would break through the rules of decency, so as to shock those he conversed with, would lose the public esteem, and become incapable of doing any good" (Ibid: 30).

Hence, one could derive from the work of Montesquieu two important factors that contribute to the Right to Communicate: the existence of a given body of regulations that can protect and maintain equality, rights and freedoms; and the importance of a democratic environment where people can exercise the freedom to choose representatives who will in turn contribute to the law and the protection of liberty. Although acknowledging his contribution to this legal realization of the Right to Communicate, one must also criticize his differentiation between the two kinds of liberties (political and philosophical) and question why he allows thinkers to freely express their opinions and criticism in the civil realm while he regards the same freedom as breaking laws when criticizing the political system.

Voltaire (1694–1778): Absolute Freedom of Speech

Voltaire's (1694–1778) skepticism offers a good explanation of diversity and normative standards in applying rules, as he initially questions everything rationally, motivated by a sincere belief in the liberty of the mind and persons.

Voltaire is considered to be one of the greatest advocates for an absolute Right to Communicate. In one of his famous political writings The *ABC Dialogues: Seventeen,* imaginary conversations occur between three persons of different mental and philosophical positions: *A*, the Englishman, free, but with a confident personality; *B*, may be Voltaire himself; and *C*, a Dutch man. These conversations dealt with many different "controversial" topics: law, religion, freedom, toleration, war, and legislations, among others.

Two of these conversations require further analysis as they are found to be crucial in the Right to Communicate debate proposed in this book. The first is the ninth conversation on the *serfdom of minds*:

B: What do you think about slavery of the mind?
A: What do you mean by slavery of the mind?
B: I mean that practice whereby the minds of our children are shaped just like Caribbean women knead the heads of their children; whereby their mouths are first thought to mumble nonsense which we ourselves ridicule; whereby they are made to believe nonsense as soon as they start believing . . . lastly, the practice whereby laws are passed stopping men from writing, talking and even thinking.

(Voltaire, 1768: 139)

It is clear from this excerpt that Voltaire highly esteems freedom of the mind as the primary medium of communication. He is criticizing and attacking different forms of censorship and violations of the people's right to know and communicate. He considers educating, speaking, and believing "nonsense" as one form the violation of human mind. Then, contradicting Montesquieu, he says that in order to have a certain right to communicate our own ideas, communication should not be subject of the laws that regulate authorship, printing, and speech among other communication media. Evidently, in passages such as the following, Voltaire attacked those who argued for censorship of books that contained controversies and could threaten religion or political power:

> In general, we have as natural a right to make use of our pens as of our tongue, at our peril, risk, and hazard. I know many books which have bored their readers, but I know of none which has done real evil. Theologians, or pretended politicians, cry: "Religion is destroyed, the government is lost, if you print certain truths or certain paradoxes. Never dare to think, till you have asked permission from a monk or a clerk. It is against the public welfare for a man to think for himself.
>
> (cited in Salvadori, 1972: 64)

Regarding freedom of communication, one can argue that Voltaire was one of the greatest advocates of the liberty of the press during the eighteenth century, a conviction derived from his belief in personal liberty given by nature. For him, freedom of speech is absolute. He believes that humans should enjoy speaking their ideas through their own will without any constraints. The conversation progresses:

> C: But it's a good thing that everyone does not speak his mind. You should not insult by what you write, or what you say, those laws under whose protection you enjoy your wealth, your freedom, and all the comforts of life.
>
> A: Of course not, and reckless traitors must be punished; but because writing can be abused, must men be forbidden to do it? . . . people are robbed in the streets, must they be forbidden from walking in them because of that? People say stupid and insulting things, but must speaking be forbidden?
>
> (Voltaire, 1768: 140)

He continues highlighting his thoughts through this imaginary dialogue, arguing that people cannot simply justify censoring all kinds of communication as a result of some "bad" practices. This notion was also asserted by Milton when he argued every true Christian has to make his own choices when all books are available, "good" and also "bad." Importantly, Voltaire, through his imaginary Dutchman C, is raising the "toleration" principle in communication:

> C: Everybody can write what they think in my country at their own risk; it's the only way to speak to one's country. If it finds that you have spoken foolishly, it boos you; if seditiously, it punishes you; if wisely and nobly, it loves you and rewards you . . . Without the freedom to explain what one thinks, there is no freedom among men.
>
> (Ibid)

According to a recent study, Voltaire's thought, like that of many eighteenth century intellectuals, emphasizes a general rejection of intolerance or violence in human actions, a position which could be seen as preliminary to the idea of human rights. In his *Traité sur la Tolérance*, he "offers a catalogue of man's inhumanity to man," according to Bordas (2003:15), and speaks out passionately for an end to this form of human brutality: "The right of intolerance is therefore absurd and barbaric: it is the right of tigers, and it is indeed hideous, because the only reason tigers destroy is in order to eat, whereas we have exterminated one another for a paragraph" (Ibid: 24).

From this excerpt, it is clear that Voltaire was supporting a universal right to free expression, evident in his criticism of intolerance. He believes that we, as human beings, are struggling with our differences and conflicts, but alternatively, he sees tolerance principle as the only solution: "Discord . . . is very striking lesson that we should pardon each other's errors. Discord is the great ill of mankind, and tolerance is the only remedy for it" (cited in Salvadori, 1972: 68).

On Religion is another example of Voltaire's conversations that are relevant in this historical exploration of intellectual thought about communication as a human right. In this conversation, Voltaire explicitly expresses, in a quote that worth citing in length, his thoughts about a right to communicate one's ideas, thoughts, and opinions, even if they are representing criticism to political, and religious powers in society:

C: Do you wish to see anything printed about government and religion?

A: Whoever keeps silent on these two subjects, whoever cannot look closely at these two polarities of human life, is just a coward . . . our pen is the first weapon against tyranny, and our sword the second.

C: What! Writing against the religion of your country!

B: Ah! You're not thinking, Mr. C. IF the first Christians had not been free to write against the religion of the Roman Empire, they would never have established their own. . . Why do you want to deprive us of the freedom they had?

C: God save me from outlawing that precious freedom! But I want to see some tact in it, as in decent conversation; everyone says what he thinks, but no-one insults the whole company.

A: I am not asking you to insult society either, but to enlighten it. if a country's religion is scared. A hundred thousand volumes written against it will do it no more harm than o rock-solid walls by a hundred thousand snowballs.

(Voltaire, 1768: 142–143)

In this dialogue, Voltaire makes a clear and strong position for a possible Right to Communicate. First, he asserts the individual freedom to express one's own opinions and thoughts freely and without frontiers, then, he significantly suggests that this freedom should be channeled to the well being of the society as a whole.

Based on Voltaire's previous interpretation, it can be argued that he perceived the Right to Communicate more widely than Milton to include freedom to think, express, publish, and criticize his ideas and thoughts. Secondly, he agrees on the importance and necessity of freedom and liberty in human life. It is interesting to mention here that although he is considered an advocate for human rights, he was accused of gender-based criticism from the feminist perspective, which could be seen as not believing in the universal Right to Communicate. Rivière, for example, says that his general evaluation of women's writings and literature was "derogatory," and that he was "far from complimentary towards women," whether they were intellectuals, artists, or celebrities. She claims that this was due to "his egocentric approach, and to the androcentric values typical of the male-dominated interpretative community of his day; he was insensitive to what really mattered to women and refused to connect with women writers" (2001: 6). Despite this criticism, he is still regarded as one of the great early thinkers who believed in the absolute freedom of speech, and hence, a Right to Communicate.

In the following historical period, the thoughts of great thinkers like Jean Jacques Rousseau (1712–1778) and Immanuel Kant (1724–1804) have been nourishing the thought of communication as human right indirectly through their assertion on the principles of democracy, freedom, liberty, equality, morality, and significantly, duty.

Jeremy Bentham (1748–1832): Public Opinion and Freedom of Expression

As a liberal utilitarian, Jeremy Bentham (1748–1832) was an important advocate for the Right to Communicate, as he saw public opinion, one form of communication, as an important tool to investigate and judge the actions of government. He balanced the duty of informing the public of government politics and actions on the press or newspapers and mediating between the public and the government. Hence, freedom of the press was a crucial point in his theory of the "Public Opinion Tribunal"—as Cutler's suggests—as a social institution that judges and assesses the political powers in a society.

The significance of this contribution should not be underestimated. As there are some studies that assert the influence of Bentham's conception of the "Public Opinion Tribunal" on the thoughts of German philosopher, Jürgen Habermas for example, particularly, the way he synthesized the importance and evolution of the public sphere as one form of "rational communicative critical discourse in a democratic environment" (Cutler, 1999: 323). Bentham's philosophy could be seen then as relaying on the importance of freedom of the press and free expression among individuals of ideas, thoughts, and opinions on the one hand; and moreover, the type of communication, its direction, its uses and its flow on the other hand. Bentham does not accept that the political powers in societies should censor newspapers that inform the people of what is happening, nor does he accept that the direction of communication flow should be one way—from authorities to the public.

In other words, Bentham first provides an early conception of the public sphere, and second, a larger and new rational of why we, as human beings, might have a Right to Communicate. As through the exercise of free speech and opinions in the public sphere, individuals can assess and criticize public policy and contribute positively to public life. Bentham's model of communication and democracy called for an open, two-way channel. John Stuart Mill explains the significance of the public opinion and its role in society for Bentham:

> [Bentham] exhausted all the resources of ingenuity in devising means for riveting the yoke of public opinion closer and closer round the necks of all

> public functionaries, . . . Wherever all the forces of society act in one single direction, the just claims of the individual human being are in extreme peril. The power of the majority is salutary so far as it is used defensively, not offensively—as its exertion is tempered by respect for the personality of the individual, and deference to superiority of cultivated intelligence.
>
> (Mill, 1867: 168)

Generally, a one-way system of communication would not represent Bentham's understanding of the Right to Communicate. While his "Tribunal" has more than one function, the most important one is that all persons should enjoy the right of access to information. In other words, as a believer in rational progressivism, he regards public opinion as mainly formed within a system where there is a free flow of information throughout the society. With such free access, Bentham believed, people would choose the opinion or the position that provided them with the "greatest happiness" (Cutler, 1999: 340–343).

As for his approach to rights, however, Bentham rejects the possibility of moral or natural rights per se, claiming that they are "nonsense." Here he explains that the "want" does not constitute a "right":

> In proportion to the want of happiness resulting from the want of rights, a reason exists for wishing that there were such things as rights. But reasons for wishing there were such things as rights, are not rights; a reason for wishing that a certain right were established, is not that right—want is not supply—hunger is not bread. That which has no existence cannot require anything to preserve it from destruction.
>
> (cited in Palumbo, 1982: 122)

Bentham supports legal rights, as they are, representing a stronger obligation and protection than being vague, as the case of natural rights. He clarifies:

> Natural Rights is simply nonsense: natural and imprescriptible rights, rhetorical nonsense, nonsense upon stilts. But this rhetorical nonsense ends in the old strain of mischievous nonsense: for immediately a list of these pretended natural rights is given, and those are so expressed as to present to view legal rights. And of these rights, whatever they are, there is not, it seems, any one of which any government can, upon any occasion whatever, abrogate the smallest particle.
>
> (Ibid)

Though Bentham could be regarded a contributor to the thought of communication as a human right through his early assertion on the public sphere's role in society, and the importance of the freedom of expression and the public opinion in society, it is argued that one could not justify the claim of a Right to Communicate according to the "greatest happiness," as he argues. Indeed, the quantitative method is not the only justification of a claim of a right. Finally, John Stuart Mill pays tribute to the significance of Bentham's doctrine, speaking out for freedom of expression and his leadership in the movement for the recognition of thoughts' exchange that was elaborated later as one of the basic human rights in his *Bentham*, published in 1867 in a collection of essays, *Dissertations and Discussions*. It is apparent that he esteemed Bentham as a philosopher and key thinker:

> If we were asked to say, in the fewest possible words, what we conceive to be Bentham's place among these great intellectual benefactors of humanity; . . . we should say—he was not a great philosopher, but he was a great reformer in

philosophy. . . . He introduced into morals and politics those habits of thought and modes of investigation, which are essential to the idea of science; . . . It was not his opinions, in short, but his method, that constituted the novelty and the value of what he did.

(Mill, 1867: 138)

Strongly influenced by Bentham's philosophy, John Stuart Mill's position advocates for a right to communicate if it meets specific prerequisites, the relative moral consequences of this right.

John Stuart Mill (1806-1873): Absolute Right Relative to Greatest Happiness

Another important contribution to the development of the concept of communication as an important human right is that of John Stuart Mill (1806–1873). Mill offers a good explanation of the concepts of freedom and the rightness of action in many of his works. In his *Utilitarianism*, for example, he explains these conceptions, suggesting that the highest goal of freedom and moral action is to "promote the greatest happiness of the greatest number"; therefore, he is stating a sort of normative standard of how humans can judge a specific action. Mill differs from Bentham, who distinguished pleasures only in quantity, in qualifying happiness or pleasures as higher or lower, superior or inferior, and thus more or less valuable. Following this approach, and in developing his own definition of morality, Mill constructed a theory of moral standards based on utility (which is useful in this context of discovering the Right to Communicate); that is, utilitarian action as the basis for defining a normative degree of morality. Mill, in his essay *On Liberty*, of which a large part is dedicated to the discussion of freedom of thought and expression, conceptualizes "liberty" as a virtue necessary for happiness. As Gary explains, "The principle of utility is an evaluative and not an action-guiding principle and direct utilitarian policy is condemned as self-defeating . . . Mill develops in that essay . . . a conception in which happiness has a link with liberty" (1988, p. 122). Thus, one could infer from this and the passage hereunder that Mill's approach to the Right to Communicate could be seen as the rightness or goodness of the action is determined by its consequences:

> The morality of an action depends on its foreseeable consequences; its beauty, and its lovableness, or the reverse, depend on the qualities which it is evidence of. Thus a lie is *wrong*, because its effect is to mislead, and because it tends to destroy the confidence of man in man; it is also *mean*, because it is cowardly—because it proceeds from not daring to face the consequences of telling the truth.
>
> (Mill, 1867: 172)

In other words, the weight of an action itself, whether it leads to a positive consequence or not, is not as important as whether this action leads to the "greatest happiness" for the greatest number of people while minimizing for others.

Mill argues for the freedom of thought as an inseparable human right, and at the same time promotes the importance of individuality, emphasizing the treatment of one's opinion as one's own "personal property." This apparently unlimited freedom is not, in fact, the freedom to express "heretical" statements and opinions; rather, Mill suggests that freedom of thought and opinion could be channeled into the well-being of society as a whole through the individual ability to criticize the "corrupt" government. This idea of democracy, where citizens can effectively express their opinions and get involved in social decision-making, includes the right of the minority to be heard; one of the core contemporary debates in the international human rights' sphere:

> If all mankind minus one were of one opinion, and only one person were of the contrary opinion, mankind would be no more justified in silencing that one person, than he, if he had the power, would be justified in silencing mankind. Were an opinion a personal possession of no value except to the owner, if to be obstructed in the enjoyment of it were simply a private injury, it would make some difference whether the injury was inflicted only on a few persons or on many. But the peculiar evil of silencing the expression of an opinion is, that it is robbing the human race; posterity as well as the existing generation; those who dissent from the opinion, still more than those who hold it.
>
> (Mill, 1859: 76)

From this excerpt of *On Liberty*, one can see that Mill (1859) is advocating for the individual right to free speech without constraint, through his/her right not to be silenced. Paradoxically, does this statement advocate an absolute right to speech, whatever the consequences are, or does Mill believe in the individual's capability of practicing a "good" pattern of communication and speech, and as such, s/he could not be silenced?

In the fourth chapter of his *On Liberty*, Mill asserts the right of individuals to seek their freedom; at the same time, however, they are bound by a moral rule and utilitarian guideline of bringing happiness and preventing harm to other individuals. In other words, individuals in practicing their rights should also respect the rights of others individuals to act differently and freely. In this context, questions of the relation between the individual and society inevitably arise:

> Though society is not founded on a contract, . . . everyone who receives the protection of society owes a return for the benefit, and the fact of living in society renders it indispensable that each should be bound to observe a certain line of conduct toward the rest. This conduct consists, first, in not injuring the interests of one another, or rather certain interests which, either by express legal provision or by tacit understanding, ought to be considered as rights.
>
> (Ibid: 141)

Though much credit is given to Mill's contribution to the concept of liberty, critics argue that there is some difficulty in applying it practically: "Application of the Principle of Liberty . . . is useless in guiding policy about the restraint of liberty" (Gray, 1988: 123). Also, Mill does not provide guidelines for an objective judgment of the liberty principle; he does not tell us, for instance, "how much liberty is required" or "how much harm prevention" is needed (Ibid: 124).

Although Mill's philosophy may be interpreted differently, owing to confusion over the limits of a given right, he makes it clear that everyone as an "individual human" is free to exercise freedom of speech under one condition, which is related not to the content, as O'Rourke argues, but to the "circumstances" in which the opinion is expressed (2001: 126–127). Mill sets out those limits in the third chapter of *On Liberty* where he declares that it is essential to look to the speech's consequences and its harmful effects on others and not the speech in itself as a "harmful act":

> No one pretends that actions should be as free as opinions. On the contrary, even opinions lose their immunity when the circumstances in which they are expressed are such as to constitute their expression a positive instigation to some mischievous act . . . Acts, of whatever kind, which without justifiable cause do harm to others may be,

> and in the more important cases absolutely require to be, controlled by the unfavourable sentiments, and, when needful, by the active interference of mankind. The liberty of the individual must be thus far limited; he must not make himself a nuisance to other people.
>
> (Mill, 1859: 119)

Here, Mill is clearly arguing that an act (like publishing pornography for example) that causes harm to people should be eliminated at once. Therefore, he is saying that freedom of opinions is not absolute until it meets with the social and moral relative requirement in order to accept it.

In fact, the following Millian explanation of what he considers to be a "right" is significantly important in this historical exploration, as it resembles, to a great extent, what Hohfeld had offered in the provisional conceptualization of a "right." He says:

> When we call anything a person's right, we mean that he has a valid claim on society to protect him in the possession of it, either by the force of law, or by that of education and opinion. If he has what we consider a sufficient claim, or whatever account, to have something guaranteed to him by society, we say that he has a right to it.
>
> (Mill, 1861: 326)

Therefore, Mill is clearly arguing that to possess a right, such as the Right to Communicate for example, is to have a strong claim to the extent of being protected by society against any violation. Mill's position brings about an objection in the fact that he refers to "utility" to be the credible reason for claiming this right, though, he previously declared favour over moral reasons that are clearly representing a stronger claim than the utility reasons. He clarifies his position: "To have a right, then, is, I conceive, to have something which society ought to defend me in the possession of. If the objector goes on to ask why it ought, I can give him no other reason than general utility" (Ibid: 326).

In the context of the ideas discussed and this endeavour to explore the roots of the concept of the "Right to Communicate," the following example correlates and merges these ideas to apply them to the Right to Communicate. Consider one of the problems discussed in Chapter 3, that of child-murderer Clifford Olson, or publishing online pornography, for example. Then imagine how Milton, Locke, Voltaire, and Mill would apply their philosophies to that situation.

Given the time variable in this recent case, if Olson's diaries are considered a "bad book"m, it is fair to say that Milton would initially allow him to publish his memoir as to give the true Christian believer the choice to choose between "good" and "evil," however, he would also raise the "burning-book principle" against the memoir after it had been published. Again, Milton, through his philosophy, does not provide a specific guideline of how this person can be judged and whether he can claim his Right to Communicate freely through his paradox of pre and post censorship allowance. Still the question remains: Would Milton accept child pornography as a form of free communication?

Kant would say that the action of publishing a murderer's diary is in itself is immoral, therefore this murderer cannot make his claim for freedom of expression on the basis of an absolute and universal right. Mill would agree with Kant, but for different reasons. He would assume that this person has the right to publish his diaries, but would ask certain questions. What is the utility of them to the whole society? Would the publication of these diaries achieve the greatest degree of happiness for the greatest number of people, and minimize harm to the society? Is this person claiming freedom of speech, and if so, what are the consequences of their "harmful act"?[4]

Mill would refuse this murderer's claim for his Right to Communicate because no good or happiness would be accomplished and harm to some would certainly result from publishing his gruesome memoirs. In this regard, he upholds that:

> There are many acts which, being directly injurious only to the agents themselves, ought not to be legally interdicted, but which, if done publicly, are a violation of good manners and, coming thus within the category of offenses against others, may rightly be prohibited. Of this kind are offences against decency; on which it is unnecessary to dwell, the rather as they are only connected indirectly with our subject, the objection to publicity being equally strong in the case of many actions not in themselves condemnable, nor supposed to be so.
>
> (Mill, 1859: 168)

As for Voltaire, it is likely that he would propose that Olson could publish his book on the basis of the absolute right to speech on the one hand, and as a way to tolerate him on the other. Voltaire maintains that: "I disapprove of what you say but I will defend to the death your right to say it" (cited in Lee, 1990: 3).

From this history of intellectual contributions, from Milton to Mill, one can see that although their philosophies are nourishing the idea of communication as a human right, they do not offer a comprehensive approach to the problems and controversies previously discussed in this book which stem from the claim for an absolute Right to Communicate. The following is an illustration of the contributions of contemporary intellectuals on this debate who argue that they offer a plausible theorization of communication as a "human right."

Notes

1. Kendall describes Milton's aristocratic character through an analysis of one of his famous verses:
   This is true liberty when free born man
   Having to advise the public, may speak free;
   Which he who can, and will, deserves high praise,
   Who neither can nor will, may hold his peace,
   What can better juster in a state like this? (cited in Kendall, 1960: 456).
   Look to the words "who can and will" to describe the "free man" who can advise the public, while the words "neither can nor will" to describe others who cannot. Here, Milton describes the man who can speak freely and publicly as representing the true kind of liberty.

2. See also, Bob Chase in "John Locke and cultural relativism," argues: "Locke is both a founding theorist of empiricism and a political thinker devoted to the rational defense of individual property rights" (1997: 61).

3. A close examination of Locke's conception of "language" in the *Essay* gives a sense of how he regards it as an important medium of communication: "Language is 'the great conduit'" (cited in Peters, 1999: 84). Other studies, such as that of Bob Chase (1997: 72) argue in favour of the idea that Locke was a defender of "linguistic relativism," as he affirms first the non-divine origins of language, referring to "man" as the "language creator" on the one hand, and the individuality of language on the other. Therefore, Chase states, Locke is arguably implying the differences between humans in expressing their ideas through different "linguistic" formats.

4. I quote from the murdered children's parents' appeal to the Federal Solicitor General Kaplan: "We are suffering further injury at present from the knowledge that Clifford Olson has benefited financially from the murder of our children. This is further aggravated by the fact that Mr. Olson may benefit yet again through publication of his disgusting, wicked, perverted story. Clifford Olson derives obvious personal delight at the publicity that has been given him and knows no moral boundary that will prevent him from collecting financially, either directly or indirectly, for the sale of his memoirs." For further details concerning this story, see: http://www.crimelibrary.com/serial_killers/predators/olson/20.html?sect=2.

Chapter 5

Toward a Theorization of Communication as a "Human Right"

> Freedom of inquiry, toleration of diverse views, freedom of communication, the distribution of what is found out to every individual the ultimate intellectual consumer, are involved in the democratic as in the scientific method.
>
> *(Dewey, 1939: 102)*

> Speech act may be called "acceptable" if it satisfies the conditions that are necessary in order that the hearer be allowed to take a "yes" position on the claim raised by the speaker. These conditions cannot be satisfied one-sidedly, either relative to the speaker or to the hearer.
>
> *(Habermas, 1984: 298)*

> It is imperative today to consider the general role of technology not only as an instrument for effectuating cultural domination but as an embodiment of this very domination.
>
> *(Schiller, 1976: 47)*

Although several international declarations have proclaimed communication as a basic and universal right for all human beings without any kind of qualification, there are many kinds of communication that make these proclamations indeed problematic. As previously outlined, early discussion regarding communication by Milton, Locke, Voltaire, and Mill generally recognized such problematic cases, however, it is questionable whether they provided a satisfactory way of resolving the difficulties raised, especially given the vast media of communication used in our contemporary society. This chapter examines two recent thinkers—John Dewey and Jürgen Habermas—to see whether their philosophies offer a more helpful approach to the dilemmas in question and provide a sounder basis for considering communication as a human right. To that end, it will further conclude, by an analysis of one more contemporary understanding of communication as a human right to communicate, not only information, rather as a right to communicate cultures through the work of Herbert Schiller on media and cultural imperialism.

John Dewey (1864–1952): Communication as a Social Dialogue

John Dewey (1864–1952) was an American pragmatist, moral philosopher, and anchor of the Chicago School. His philosophy and contributions to the field of communication studies are useful in resolving some of the debates and problems examined in Chapter 3, and help to define a possible Right to Communicate in the twentieth century.

Before discussing whether communication could be considered as a human right according to the Deweyian philosophy, it is instructive to begin first with Dewey's perspective and conceptualization of "communication." Essentially, communication for Dewey is a core component in the structure of society; without its full existence, society lacks liberty, freedom, and most importantly, democracy. He wrote the following, plainly illustrating the role of communication in society:

> Society exists through a process of transmission quite as much as biological life. This transmission occurs by means of communication of habits of doing, thinking, and feeling from the older to the younger, without this communication of ideals, hopes, expectations, standards, opinions, from those members of society who are passing out of the group life to those who are coming into it, social life could not survive.
>
> (Dewey, 1916: 3)

Dewey's notion of communication is widely related to the existence of human beings in a "community." He believes that as long as humans co-exist, they have to communicate using several media. In fact, he relates communication to a trio-relationship that consists of common, communication, and community dimensions. Dewey explains that human beings share many aspects of life when they live together in a community, and as such, communication is their tool to exchange feelings, language, attitudes, and opinions:

> Society not only continues to exist *by* transmission, *by* communication, but it may fairly be said to exist *in* transmission, *in* communication, there is more than a verbal tie between the words common, community, and communication. Men live in a community in virtue of the things which they have in common; and communication is the way in which they come to possess things in common.
>
> (Ibid, *emphasis in original*)

Within this context, Dewey highlights the significance of public participation, using communication in social life. We can infer from this that he may include freedom of expression and freedom of speech as basic requirements in this process: "Each would have to know what the other was about and would have to have some way of keeping the other informed as to his own purpose and progress. Consensus demands communication" (Dewey, 1916: 4). Moreover, he conceives of communication not only as a channel to transmit messages, but also as a social institution that produces values in society. He asserts the importance of the social environment where participants exchange their information, ideas and other types of messages "equally": "In order to have a large number of values on continuity, all the members of the group must have an equable opportunity to receive and to take from others" (Ibid: 84).

At the same time, Dewey asserts that communication should have certain conditions in order to function the way he suggests as he sees communication as a social conversation between participants within a society, not merely sending and receiving messages. He argues that, "Freedom of inquiry, toleration of diverse views, freedom of communication, the distribution of what is found out to every individual the ultimate intellectual consumer, are involved in the democratic as in the scientific method" (Dewey, 1939: 102).

Given Dewey's conception of communication as social thinking, one could classify him as a defender of communication as a basic human right. Indeed, he criticizes the totalitarian regimes that used propaganda as a tool of manipulating the public in societies like the Second World War in Germany, for example. Here, we can raise the question proposed in Chapter 3 once again concerning the practice of propaganda and whether totalitarian regimes can claim the absolute right to communicate their destructive ideas when they are backed by the various declarations that have stated that communication is a right without further qualification. Dewey argues that propaganda could never be considered as communication and, accordingly, cannot be claimed as a universal or absolute right:

> Dictatorship exercises complete command over the press, over travel, over letters and personal communications, in consequence, only a few have access to the sources of information about political methods, and that few is the group with the greatest interest in preventing free inquiry and report. This suppression of freedom of belief and of speech, press and assembly is not among the facts in dispute for it is of the essence of the dictatorship.
>
> (Ibid: 90)

Thus, we can infer from this that the practice of propaganda is simply not considered communication, because it is not the production of a social conversation between individuals in society. Rather, it is merely the empowerment of a small group or individual on different resources of information. It is communication in society on one hand, yet in disregard of the individual's will on the other. Clearly, the majority of individuals do not have the option of free inquiry and free speech under this system of totalitarianism.

Another important dimension in Dewey's philosophy that enriched our discovery of a possible right to communicate is his concepts of "freedom," and "democracy." For Dewey, freedom means "individuality," where individuals practice their will and more importantly their rationality:

> The idea of freedom has been connected with the idea of individuality, of *the* individual. The connection has been so close and often reiterated that it has come to seem inherent . . . yet the affiliation of the idea of freedom is with the idea of rationality. Those are free who govern themselves by the dictates of reason; those who follow the promptings of appetite and sense are ruled by them as to be unfree.
>
> (Ibid: 24)

Thus, even with his recognition of the importance of the individuals' practice of free communication, their practice within the social system is superior for him. He says that, "When this identification [identifying the social order in society] is established, it follows that any merely individual right must yield to the general welfare" (Dewey, 1935: 65–66). In other words, freedom of speech, as one of the individual liberties, is not absolute in practice, according to Dewey. Consider the case of a murderer's autobiography. One could propose the question of whether he is practicing his freedom rationally and according to the established social norms, values, and morals. Dewey would argue against his right to communicate. The following extract of Dewey's *Liberalism and Social Action* (1935) clearly outlines the boundaries of a possible Right to Communicate. He begins by illustrating the main principles of the American revolutionaries who brought forward the *Declaration of Independence*, by saying:

> Those who won our independence believed that freedom to think as you will and to speak as you think are means indispensable to the discovery and spread of political truth; that without free speech and assembly discussion would be futile; that with them, discussion affords ordinarily adequate protection against the dissemination of noxious doctrines; that the greatest menace to freedom is an inert people; that public discussion is a political duty.
>
> (Ibid: 66)

He continues by saying that it is not adequate to conceive of freedom of speech according to previous revolutionary doctrine without taking into account the various established social norms and values produced in a given society:

> The public function of free individual thought and speech is clearly recognized in the words quoted. But the reception of the truth of the words is met

> by an obstacle: the old habit of defending liberty of thought and expression as something inhering in individuals apart from and even in opposition to social claims.
>
> (Ibid: 67)

Finally, it is useful to highlight the importance of the second Deweyian ideal: "democracy." Some believe that democracy allows people to practice communication by advocating principles such as freedom of speech and the open exchange of opinions and thoughts. In fact, Dewey supports the opposite position: he considers communication to be the essential tool for the practice of democracy. Kallen says that both democracy and science represent, according to Dewey, the "scara, or the sancta of the common faith, a faith that brings together all the world's religions on equal terms of peace and freedom . . . it is the religion of the free mind and the open heart" (1950, p. 175).[1] Dewey objected to the narrowly tailored conceptualization of democracy as a form of political organization. For him, democracy is simply a way of social *life*:

> A democracy is more than a form of government; it is primarily a mode of associated living, of conjoint communicated experience. The extension in space of the number of individuals who participate in an interest so that each has to refer his action to that of others, and to consider the action of others to give point and direction to his own, is equivalent to the breaking down of those barriers of class, race, and national territory which kept men from perceiving the full import of their activity.
>
> (Dewey, 1916: 87)

As a moral philosopher, he placed more importance on the ethical dimension of this concept than a superficial glance at it. Thus, in the context of finding an appropriate approach to understanding a possible Right to Communicate, the practice of democracy in the sense of Deweyian interpretation—where every member of society expresses his ideas, thoughts, and opinions freely and, more importantly, according to the social order—is closely related to a possible Right to Communicate. Peters quotes Dewey in his *The Ethics of Democracy:*

> [Democracy] is a form of moral and spiritual association . . . it is the form of society in which every man [or woman] has a chance and knows that he [she] has it—and we may add, a chance to which no possible limits can be put, a chance which is truly infinite, the chance to become a person . . . Democracy is an ethical idea, the idea of a personality, with truly infinite capacities, incorporate with every man [woman]. Democracy and the one, the ultimate, ethical ideal of humanity are to my mind synonyms.
>
> (Peters, 1989: 204)

Synthesizing the perspectives discussed above, one could argue that Dewey asserts that the Right to Communicate is a human right, believing that individuals would choose to use their freedom of speech toward suitable ends, such as democracy and the well being of the whole society. Moreover, communication, employed ethically, is the most important tool to achieve and maintain democracy, where people exercise freedom of speech and exchange opinions and ideas for the benefit of society.

Jürgen Habermas (1929–): Undistorted Communication

The philosophy of Jürgen Habermas (1929–) offers two possible approaches to investigating communication as a possible human right: first, his *Theory of Communicative Action* offers a way of handling controversial practices of communication;

and second, his idea of "rational communicative discourse" may help to resolve the debate over the universality of human rights in general, and communication in particular. Habermas synthesized ideas from, and was inspired by, many intellectuals and movements that preceded him, among these were religious Protestantism, the Enlightenment, Kant, Marx, and American pragmatism,[2] especially the work of Herbert Mead and John Dewey.[3]

Habermas was greatly inspired by the Protestant culture; for him, Protestantism "gave birth to a concept of community constituted of independent moral actors bound by voluntaristic commitment to common ethical norms" (Antonio, 1989: 730). He sees Protestantism as embodying three main values: "scientific," "artistic," and "ethical," all of which form the basis for his "Universal Validity Claims (truth, beauty/ authenticity, [and] normative rightness)" (Ibid: 730–731).

At the heart of Habermas' *Theory of Communicative Action* lie two fundamental ideas: his assumption that all human speech includes what he refers to as "validity claims"; and the "Ideal Speech Situation" assumed in the use of language. Could access to pornography be considered as a Right to Communicate? Does a person have a right to use aggressive and offensive language to communicate with others, using any medium of his/her choice, such as disseminating hate speech over the Internet? What possible approaches would Habermas offer to solve these problems?

In this context, Habermas, motivated by his knowledge of psychological literature, was mainly concerned with answering the following question: "What would 'undistorted communication' be like?" (Giddens, 1985: 128). This is to some extent similar to the question proposed in this book: What type of communication could be considered universal and would be protected by the international, national, regional and even personal regulations and laws, and could such communication be considered a basic human right?

In order to answer these questions, it is important to look at Habermas' emphasis on validity claims and their being prerequisites for establishing undistorted communication between communicators. He says that in order to participate in a communicative process that aims to achieve an "understanding," one can suppose to have four basic validity claims:

> I shall develop a thesis that anyone acting communicatively must, in performing any speech action, raise universal validity claims . . . insofar as he wants to participate in a process of reaching understanding, he cannot avoid raising the following . . . validity claims. He claims to be
>
> a. *Uttering* something understandably.
> b. Giving [the hearer] *something* to understand;
> c. Making *himself* thereby understandable; and
> d. Coming to an understanding *with another person*.
>
> (Habermas, 1979: 2)

From this, one could infer that Habermas is proposing that a possible Right to Communicate is not simply "sending" messages, claiming an absolute freedom of speech whatever the content of the message represents. Instead, he is presenting the basic characteristics for an "undistorted communication" where the message-sender has specific "obligations" toward the message-receiver: that the sender speaks comprehensibly and responsibly, giving the receiver a plausible account of what he or she means.

More importantly, the speaker is justifying his speech according to specific social norms and values. Hence, one could see that hate speech, for instance, could never be considered "communication" according to Habermas. Clearly, those who voice hate speech are not, in any way, speaking truthfully, or sincerely, nor are they interpreting "true," or "justified" facts. Habermas clarifies this point:

> The speaker must choose a comprehensible expression so that speaker and hearer can understand one another, the speaker must have the intention

of communicating a true proposition content . . . so that the hearer can share the knowledge of the speaker. The speaker must want to express his intentions truthfully so that the hearer can believe.

(Ibid: 2)

Giddens summarizes this position by explaining that for Habermas, "undistorted communication is language-use in which speakers can defend all four validity-claims—where what is said can be shown to be meaningful, true, justified and sincere" (1985: 129). Hence, in Habermas' view, the controversies and problems discussed in Chapter 3, such as hate speech, offensive language, and criminal diaries, could not be protected under the claim of the absolute or universal right of communication, because, lacking the Habermasian pre-conditions discussed above, these practices are not communication. Deception, manipulation, and cheating, among communicators, are certainly part of what he meant by "distorted communication."

Also, it is important to clarify the significance of the "obligation" dimension in Habermas' point of view. The speaker, according to him, must meet specific obligations that the hearer is expecting to be fulfilled. For Habermas, "The bond into which the speaker is willing to enter with the performance of an illocutionary act means a guarantee that, in consequence of his utterance, he will fulfill certain conditions" (Habermas, 1979: 62). Considering the previous Habermasian explanation, it can be argued that his communication prerequisites were, interestingly, the main argument of the New World Information Order debate during in the 1970s. The problems of sending/receiving on the one hand, and right/obligation on the other, were central to the Third World and developing countries discussion. Massmoudi explains:

Freedom of information is presented as the corollary of freedom of opinion and freedom of expression, but was in fact conceived as the freedom of the informing agent. As a result, it has become an

> instrument of domination in the hands of those who control the media. In legal terms, it has resulted in the enshrining of the rights of the communicator, while disregarding his duties and responsibilities towards those to whom he is communicating.
>
> (1990: 313)

Accordingly, developing countries believe that they are only receiving "unacceptable" messages, sometimes thought to be "problematic" for their culture, norms, traditions, and social values as well. This belief is the reason behind their claims for a more balanced information flow. Habermas genuinely set up these claims by his notion of "reciprocal" communication, where a sender (or speaker) may have a right to send, but under the condition that he or she meets the receiver's demands and expectations:

> The speaker must choose an utterance that is right so that the hearer can accept the utterance and speaker and hearer can agree with one another in the utterance with respect to a recognized normative background. Moreover, communicative action can continue undisturbed only as long as participants suppose that the validity claims they reciprocally raise are justified.
>
> (Habermas, 1979: 3)

Therefore, it is understood that the practice of the Right to Communicate presented in the New World Information and Communication Order (NWICO) debate is, in fact, only a one-sided right. The flow of information is only from the developed countries to the developing countries—or, in Habermasian terminology, from the speaker and without regard to the receiver's demands and expectations. In other words, the reciprocal communicative action does not exist in this case. With regards to another controversy raised in Chapter 3—whether Salman Rushdie could claim his right to publish a book that is not acceptable to Muslim readers on the basis of his right to communicate and his freedom of speech—Habermas sets out another condition:

> Speech act may be called "acceptable" if it satisfies the conditions that are necessary in order that the hearer be allowed to take a "yes" position on the claim raised by the speaker. These conditions cannot be satisfied one-sidedly, either relative to the speaker or to the hearer.
>
> (Habermas, 1984: 298)

One can argue accordingly that Rushdie was not the only participant in this communicative situation, but there are other communicators: the hearers or readers of his book who did not take a "yes" position from his speech. On the contrary, some receivers did not accept his speech because it did not fulfill their demands or his "right" to communicate. A possible answer to the previous question is that Rushdie does not have an absolute Right to Communicate, but a right that is bound by his duties toward recipients of his speech to be just, true, justified and importantly, "acceptable."

Given these validity claims, in reference to another problem raised concerning whether pornographers have the absolute Right to Communicate, it can be seen that the Habermasian validity claims are lacking. No one could argue in Habermas' terms, then, that published pornographic materials (as messages), are "right" and that the content is "true," that pornography represents "truth," or that pornography is "justified" as being in line with and in accordance with social rights and norms.

Habermas, in other words, emphasizes the conjunction between the "claim" or the expression and its "content." Therefore, advocates for hate speech, pornography, and criminal autobiographies cannot claim the protection of the law as they are not practicing communication in this sense.

Here, Habermas clarifies that the content of the sender's speech is a very important variable that leads the receiver to either accept or reject it:

> With his "yes" the speaker accepts a speech-act offer and grounds an agreement; this agreement concerns the *content of the utterance,* on the one hand, and, on the other hand, certain *guarantees immanent to speech acts* and certain *obligations relevant to the sequel of interaction.*
>
> (Ibid: 296, *emphasis in original*)

Collectively, we can summarize the Habermasian contribution in the thought of communication as a possible human right through his assertion of both "responsibility" and "rationality." First, responsibility, as clarified before, is the obligation that makes the speaker committed to the receiver of providing him with a pure, true, and sincere pattern of communication. This pattern, according to Habermas, leads to "understanding," and as such, we can eliminate the problems raised in Chapter 3 as patterns of communication. Can someone claim that hate speech is aiming toward understanding rather than deceiving and manipulating? The same is applicable to pornography: Can pornographers claim that they plan to reach an understanding with receivers? In fact, Habermas summarizes his claim by pointing out that, "Only responsible persons can behave rationally. If their rationality is measured by the success of goal-directed interventions, it suffices to require that they be able to choose among alternatives and to control (some) conditions in their environment" (Habermas, 1984: 14). He also adds that validity claims are intertwined with the notion of responsibility: "In the context of communicative action, only those persons count as responsible who, as members of a communication-community, can orient their actions to intersubjectively recognized validity claims" (Ibid). As for the second Habermasian concept, "rationality," he theorizes that people are expressing their opinions and ideas for good purposes:

> Rationality is understood to be a disposition of speaking and acting subjects that is expressed in modes of behavior for which there are good reasons or grounds, this means that rational expressions admit of objective evaluation.
>
> (Ibid: 22)

Although Habermas did not clarify what exactly he meant by "good reasons," one could predict that they might be the positive claims of communication according to certain social norms and values. The example of the murderer's autobiography illustrates Habermas' meaning. In fact, Habermas' prerequisites for undistorted communication through his validity claims are also useful in analyzing whether the murderer has a Right to Communicate or not. Habermas asserts that it is not sufficient to provide a justification for the communicator's position—such as Clifford Olson, for example—but it is important to establish the validity claims within certain social contexts such as social norms and values in a given society. Habermas specifies:

> In contexts of communicative action, we call someone rational not only if he is able to put forward an assertion and, when criticized, to provide grounds for it by pointing to appropriate evidence, but also if he is following an established norm and is able, when criticized, to justify his action by explicating the given situation in the light of legitimate expectations.
>
> (Habermas, 1984: 15)

Thus, one could presume that Olson does not have a right to publish his memoirs, even though he might have certain justifications for them, such as regrettably judging his actions or attempting to reconcile with the parents of the children he murdered.

It is interesting also to note here that Habermas differentiated between two kinds of communication, depending on the validity claims: strong communication and weak communication. In the weak type of communicative action, as Heath describes it, the speakers or communicators just use the norms and values that already exist and do not aim to change them. In the strong communicative action type, on the other hand, the communicators do not just use the existing norms in society, but "generate" and produce other normative actions (2001: 30–31).

Although this is a somewhat abstract idea of communication, it implies the social role of communicators in the many levels of communication (e.g. personal, group, mass, etc.) and their responsibility for generating society's normative rules which are embodied, according to Habermas, in validity claims and moral prerequisites, including human rights. If people were to communicate using the Habermasian model of the *Ideal Speech Situation*, while practicing and producing communication as a human right, this would be the "ideal" and more powerful situation than one where the rules are merely followed without regard to the consequences (e.g. everyone has a universal right to free speech, even criminals).

In the context of the debate over whether human rights are universal or socially constructed, it is argued here that Habermas' idea of "rational communicative discourse" offers a comprehensible solution. It is important to first conceive communication in its broadest sense, including knowledge and language in general, and not to limit the concept to mass media or the press.

There is no doubt that Habermas was strongly influenced by the Enlightenment philosophers, especially the work of Kant and Marx. In his *Inclusion of the Other*, he explains the relationship between law and morality where he differentiates between the "moral universe," which includes all natural persons and hence is not limited in time or space, and the "legal community," which protects only its own members. The practice of these legal bodies lacks the "normative validity claimed by moral norms" (1999: 256). He therefore suggests that the best way to comprehend this "law" is to treat it as a "functional complement to morality." In other words, the best way to conceptualize an article in the *Universal Declaration of Human Rights* of 1948, or any other declaration that states the Right to Communicate, is as a "functional complement" of the ideal moral value that this article claims to protect, i.e., the value and importance of communication and knowledge for humans.

For Habermas, political philosophy does not really provide a balance between popular sovereignty and the rule of law. In fact, he believes that neither of the two political positions—Republicanism, derived from Aristotelian ideals, and Liberalism, derived from John Locke's ideals—can solve the problem of human rights. Instead, he proposes a "communicative" model or perspective: "a regulation [such as a human right] may claim legitimacy only if all those possibly affected by it [all nations, countries, religions, cultures, etc.] consent to it after participating in rational discourses" (Shalin, 1992: 259).

Drawing on this standpoint, one could argue that the "language" that is embodied in the *Universal Declaration of Human Rights* for the recognition and protection of the Right to Communicate is universal. According to Habermas, this regulation can claim its universal nature if all those affected by it consent to it after engaging in public, rational, and communicative discourse. Finally, as a condition to achieve this rational communicative dialogue in society, Habermas asserts the importance of a "democratic environment."

Considering the preceding discussion and the position of the third world, colonized countries in the context of Habermas' notion of a "rational communicative consensus," it must be asked how the *Universal Declaration of Human Rights* could achieve universal status while two important facts were ignored. First, that seventy countries around the world did not participate in or contribute to this rational communicative discourse, and therefore did not consent to its legitimization, acceptability, or suitability to their norms, traditions, and values. Secondly, the existing powers that consented to this declaration were at the same time colonizing those who did not!

Glendon relates that on the fiftieth anniversary of the Universal Declaration in 1998, scholars at Harvard University described the Declaration as "an arrogant attempt to universalize a particular set of ideas and to impose them upon three-quarters of the world's population, most of whom were not represented at its creation" (2001: 224).[4] Consequently, one could see that Habermas' perspective offers a fruitful resolution to this seemingly endless debate. A compelling consideration here is that, even though the claims of exclusion portray what really happened, it cannot be denied that after the decolonization of the excluded countries, and when they attained status as participants in the international body responsible for languaging their rights, one hundred and seventy countries—the entire membership of the United Nations—consented without any reservation or abstention of vote to the 1993 *Vienna Declaration*, after engaging in Habermasian "rational discourse." In the *Vienna Declaration* (1993): Article (1) clearly retains that "The universal nature of these rights and freedoms is beyond question;" and Article (5) that:

> While the significance of national and regional particularities and various historical, cultural and religious backgrounds must be borne in mind, it is the duty of States, regardless of their political, economic, and cultural systems, to promote and protect all human rights and fundamental freedoms.

In summary, human rights are universally "languaged" to include all human beings, and what is not universal is the specific context and practice of these rights. Habermas, in his *Between Facts and Norms*, clarifies:

> Actors must form an idea of this context whenever adopting the performative attitude; they want to engage successfully as citizens, representatives, judges, or officials, in realizing the system of

rights. Because these rights must be interpreted in various ways under changing social circumstances, the light they throw on this context is refracted into a spectrum of changing legal paradigms. Historical constitutions can be seen as so many ways of constructing one and the *same* practice—the practice of self-determination on the part of free and equal citizens—but like every practice this, too, is situated in history. Those involved must start with their *own current* practice if they want to achieve clarity about what such a practice means *in general*.

(1998: 386–387)

Another memorable assertion of this point was made by Charles Malik in his speech of December 9th, 1948, at the United Nations assembly on the occasion of the introduction of the *Universal Declaration of Human Rights*:

Thousands of minds and hands have helped in its formation. Every member of the United Nations has solemnly pledged itself to achieve respect for and observance of human rights. But, precisely what these rights are we were never told before . . . This is the first time the principles of human rights and fundamental freedoms are spelled out authoritatively and in precise detail. . . . I can agitate against my government, and if she does not fulfill her pledge, I shall have and feel the moral support of the entire world.

(Glendon, 2001: 164)

In conclusion, the philosophies of both Dewey and Habermas have significantly enriched the idea of a possible right to communicate. First, Dewey conceptualized communication as a special social conversation that specifies democracy, freedom of speech, and freedom of expression among its basic characteristics. Secondly, Habermas defined validity claims in which the sender of communicative message must meet the receiver's demands from him or her in order to engage with in communication. In other words, the interchangeable relationship between right-duty and demand-responsibility. Yet, it is important at this point to discuss one example which employed the conceptualization of a Right to Communicate in practice through the work of Herbert Schiller. Although representing a different intellectual standpoint than the previous two theorists, it is argued here that his critique of idea of culture imperialism and the electronic divide in our information society has flourished the understanding of communication as a human right; especially given his activism and assertion on the notion of free flow of information and the right to cultural expression using media without frontiers.

Herbert Schiller (1919-2000): A Right to Communicate Cultures

> Schiller's contribution extends well beyond his books . . . that make up his prolific scholarship. Indeed, he has also been a model of the activist scholar, what the Italian political philosopher Antonio Gramsci called "the organic intellectual," whose scholarship is mutually constituted out of civic activism.
>
> (Mosco, 2001: 196)

The work of Herbert Schiller (1919–2000) made a significant theoretical contribution to the development of the concept of the Right to Communicate, indirectly, through his comprehensive study of the issue of cultural imperialism. Historically, and before Schiller, there was no well-established and clear theoretical conceptualization of cultural imperialism, rather, there were different discourses rising from a variety of intellectuals and theorists, none of which had established a definitive definition of this term as it intertwined with the study of the Right to Communicate. Further, I will take a closer look at the work of Schiller and his contribution to the development of a unique discourse of cultural imperialism. In addition, through a brief biographical sketch, I will outline the different forces that affected him and shaped his legacy as an anti-imperialist, activist, and theorist. This chapter will also analyze Schiller's key texts, volumes that are considered to be the basis for the theory of cultural imperialism, in which it will be argued that he proposed a novel attempt to link the Right to Communicate to culture and media imperialism.

For Vincent Mosco (2001), there are two major factors that had an impact on Herbert Schiller's life, career, and ideas: the Great Depression (1929–1941), and his work for the U.S. military in Germany after the Second World War. Richard Maxwell adds a third factor: Schiller's close involvement in the developing struggle against American domination, not only in economics and politics, but also in the field of communication and information, notably through his contributions the MacBride Commission. Like many North Americans of his generation, Schiller's personality, childhood, and youth were deeply influenced by the Great Depression. He witnessed the effects of unemployment and how it negatively affected the mental and physical well-being of people: "The often dreadful memories of this period are certainly matched in number by half-forgotten episodes and ineffable events that circumscribe a life begun in the worst of times" (Maxwell, 2003: 9).

By the time he was ten years old, Schiller understood exactly how political and economic factors affect a whole society's conditions as he watched his parents struggling to manage during those difficult times. Within this framework, Herbert Schiller did not agree with many of the commonly accepted notions in American society, especially the myth of individualism as disseminated in American popular culture, particularly in Hollywood movies. Instead, he attempted to use class conflict as a key component in his personal philosophy; he says in his last published book *Living in the Number One Country: Reflections from a Critic of American Empire*, "From that time on, I loathed an economic system that could put a huge part of its workforce on the streets with no compunction . . . I have never forgotten . . . how the deprivation of work erodes human beings, those not working and those related to them" (Schiller, 2000: 12).

During the Second World War, Schiller served the U.S. military. In 1941, he worked as a junior industrial economist in the War Production Board. He then became aware of the different regulations that banned African-Americans from getting good jobs and from communicating in public spaces such as hotels and restaurants, and declared that "New York apartheid was very real" (cited in Maxwell, 2003: 14). Interestingly, in 1943, Schiller went to Morocco to work with the military where he observed the deep effects of colonization on the country's people, which further developed his understanding of the impact of socio-economic factors in global power relations. He believed that the U.S. was not in the region just as a military presence, but also as an economic and communicative one, bringing with it American consumer goods and Hollywood movies. Schiller felt this was evidence that the America was not only promoting a class division in America, but on a global scale as well.[5]

Before publishing *Mass Communication and American Empire* in 1969,[6] Schiller wrote extensively, producing many articles[7] that elaborated on his position and philosophy in the field of communication studies, which in particular opposed the predominately Lerner and Schramm "pro-Western/American" developmental paradigm—previously discussed in Chapter 2. His philosophy was shaped by his contact with the non-American perspective, particularly in Germany and Morocco, which "brought him to question American moral authority in areas of political economic organization" and instilled in him respect for the "many places that might not accept [Schramm's] assumptions and would have other ways of organizing their societies" (Maxwell, 2003: 30).

In general, in trying to position Schiller within the map of theorizing the concept of the Right to Communicate, I am arguing here that his standpoint could be seen as a combination of different discourses of cultural imperialism, not merely representing a particular, monolithic view (such as Marxist, or neo-Marxist, for example). As will be seen in the analysis of his work, his discourse of nationality was most apparent. This is logical given Schiller's role as an "activist" who was deeply inspired by the anti-colonial movement around the world from the 1950s through the 1970s. Schiller "cultivated a discourse that connected with the interests of the activist-citizen, broadly defined, rather than narrower interests of academics, however politically thoughtful, within communication studies" (Ibid: 3). During this period, many colonies became independent and started to oppose the unequal global system, not only in economics and politics, but also in the realm of access to information. For that, Schiller became occupied with the short-lived[8] efforts of these newly independent countries and their struggles against global capitalism in an effort to establish a more fertile environment for the Right to Communicate non-Western ideas, culture, and life-styles. Schiller was a also regular speaker at many forums and organizations that advocated and promoted free speech, democracy, the anti-war movement (centered in this period around the Vietnam War), as well as others who were critical of American military practices around the world.

It is clear that Schiller was also greatly influenced by Immanuel Wallerstein's World System theory,[9] which states that there is a "dynamic" relationship between the core, peripheries, and semi-peripheral areas in the world based on both power and economic relations (Mosco, 2001: 195). Mosco adds that Schiller's later work addresses even more critically the global inequality in the area of communication and information technology, in particular opposing and critiquing the utopian visions of an online world put forth by a number of scholars, most evident in his *Information Inequality* (1996). In addition, based upon the heavy criticism of the American developmental paradigm, Schiller could also be regarded as having merged the critique of modernity discourse with that of the global capitalism discourse by alerting readers to the impact of global imperialism on world cultures. In order to illustrate these claims, it is important to highlight his ideas on this particular point as it is evidently linked to the current calls for communication rights, especially with the advances of the Internet.

For the most part of his *Mass Communication and American Empire 1969*, Schiller questioned what form imperialism took as it was disseminated in the twentieth century, particularly by the United States. He asserted that although the British Empire used territorial expansion to extend and enhance its empire and exploit its economic hegemony in the colonies, it was not considered as proficient or powerful as the youthful American imperialism. Schiller was convinced that despite the decolonization of many countries after the Second World War, there was no clear evidence of their independence in reality. In the light of this claim, Schiller examined the history of American commercial broadcasting, which, he suggested, maintained a discourse of global capitalism from its inception. Contradicting Lerner and Schramm's developmental discourse, he argued that despite being a communication medium in one of the most developed countries, and one of the biggest capitalist institutions in the world, American commercial broadcasting could not be seen as offering a raw model for other countries to follow.[10] He insisted that,

> The development of broadcast communications in the United States affords perhaps the most damaging as well as the most recent evidence of how an exciting new possibility for human enlighten-

ment and satisfaction can be transformed into a stultifying swamp by a web of retrogressive social institutions.

(Schiller, 1969: 63)

Indeed, Schiller's claim that the global communication order began after the Second World War, and that the power of the American capitalist system is regarded as the new version of imperialism was not very acceptable in the Cold War climate of the 1950s and 1960s, and has been heavily criticized by some scholars.[11] Schiller added that even the academic consensus over the "death of Hobson's imperialism" is considered as a clear indication of the existence of the complex power relations that existed during that time. Hobson's theory of imperialism[12] argued that imperialism does exist in the modern time, and it has many faces, not just that of political and territorial expansion, as it manifested itself prior to the twentieth century. In order to highlight the danger Schiller felt was inherent in this particular idea; he dedicated his book, *Mass Communication and American Empire* (1969), to underlining the American communication system, its history, its purposes, and most importantly, its threat to the global communication system.

Transcending the discourse of nationality[13] and assimilating it into the critique of American imperialism, Schiller acknowledged the efforts of Frantz Fanon,[14] especially his explanation of the use of the communication media as a revolutionary tool, as exemplified by the Algerian experience. During the period of colonization, *Radio-Algiers* could be clearly defined as "Frenchmen talking to Frenchmen." After gaining independence, however, Algerian radio broadcasting was used as "a means of enlightenment, hope, and national unity, contrasted with its earlier service as a source of cultural domination and pressure," acknowledging that the radio was not just a means through which to access information, but also a tool of struggle and revolution

(Schiller, 1969: 110). Schiller added that if Fanon regarded radio broadcasting as a "revolutionary instrument," what would he had have said if he had found that the U.S. Department of Defense controlled the radio spectrum[15] and considered it as military asset? Further, Schiller argued that American imperialism extends well beyond the control of airwaves, to include the sale of equipment, program exports, and technical services contracts, among other things.

In other words, American imperialism, according to Schiller, embodies two intertwined aspects: the domination of communication resources and the different hegemonic policies that are undertaken by both the military and organizational powers. For example, Schiller identifies the American domination of satellite and radio airwaves as one example of the monopoly of the global communication resources by the U.S. On the other hand, he believes that this monopoly is underscored by the American military sponsorship of the corporate media, which in turn, disseminates American values, and markets at the same time.

In light of this analysis, Schiller, recalling his personal experience and the impact of the social and economic powers on the human life, extended his claims to the global level. He argued that the Western (including American) capitalist system and the commercialization doctrine the system adopted was dividing the globe into those who "have" and those who "have-not." After all, the "have-nots"—the developing countries—would be able to afford the new types of communication media only if they agreed to the attached condition to accept the "commercial packages which "tie" their broadcasting systems to foreign programming and foreign financial sponsorship (Ibid: 151). He added that this form of control in the field of global communication is certainly embodying (and encouraging) inequality since the giant Western transnational corporations concentrate the manufacturing, production, and transmission of cultural materials into the hands of a few, which represents certainly a danger for both cultural and media autonomy. Schiller concluded his *Mass Communication and American Empire* (1969) by maintaining that mass communication was turning out to be a

> pillar of the emergent imperial society. Messages "made in America" radiate across the globe and serve as the ganglia of national power and expansionism. The ideological images of "have-not" states are increasingly in the custody of American informational media. National authority over attitude creation and opinion formation in the developing world has weakened and is being relinquished to powerful external forces.
>
> (Ibid: 191–192)

Appraising Schiller's interpretation in this book, Hamid Mowlana, one of Schiller's students,[16] writes in his *Remembering Herbert I. Schiller*, that he established a coherent literature and some solid ground during a critical moment for future scholars to critically assess the global forces and power relations in communication studies, and notably, the importance of the Right to Communicate concept.[17] Schiller successfully illustrates that there is a problem in international communication: there is a gap between the "have" and the "have-nots" and that the role of the American corporations is to widen this gap. Hence, it becomes interesting to examine the term "culture," particularly in his book *Communication and Cultural Domination* (1976):

> *Communication Imperialism* is harsh term. It is also an unfair one in the context of the debate now going on between the Third World . . . and the First World . . . the "West." It implies that the West wants to destroy national cultures and to bring the rest of the world under its cultural . . . hegemony. These implications simply cannot be sustained by evidence.
>
> (Merrill, 1984: 176, *emphasis in original*)

The idea that communication imperialism[18] arose from Western, or more particularly American, practices in the world, as suggested in Schiller's work, has been totally rejected by scholars such as Merrill and Dennis. In general, Merrill asserts that the term imperialism implies two main actions: influence and force. He goes on to note that America's influence over the Third World's communication system should not be seen as negative action, but rather as a fact,[19] just as the Arabs influence the West (and America) with their oil; one cannot claim that "the Arabs are guilty of 'oil imperialism'" (Ibid). The term "force," however, is quite different, since imperialism denotes that a certain power is forcing subordinated people to use their communication materials. Merrill argues that the Third World is very sensitive to Western communication capabilities in the field of communications, and that is not America's problem. Secondly, and more importantly, he argues that the Third World itself is voluntarily choosing its needs, and wants from a variety of Western cultural and media materials.[20] Hence, according to Merrill, "the American system in general is pictured as 'imperialistic,' presumably *forcing* its alien factories, products, news services, and messages on staunchly resisting foreign natives. This assertion is simply false" (Ibid: 180, *emphasis in original*).

Schiller, as a result of his various visits to the developing world,[21] wrote his book *Communication and Cultural Domination* in 1976, in which he, according to Mosco, "expressed in lucid, compelling language the increasingly stark divisions in the world and the ways communication and information systems deepened and extended them" (2001: 194). This was not a quite comprehensive assessment according to Schiller's critics who believe that he "and few other have played fast and loose with the term 'imperialism' as applied to American communications agencies and to American economic enterprises" (Merrill, 1984: 179). Regardless of the importance of these two positions, either with or against Schiller, reading him, I think that Schiller's book could be considered as one of his most influential works, where he elaborated his ideas and blended the various discourses of cultural imperialism to produce a comprehensive conceptualization of cultural imperialism as a threat to the human Right to Communicate. His hypothesis was that cultural imperialism is:

> The sum of the processes by which a society is brought into the modern world and how its dominating stratum is attracted, pressured, forced, and sometimes bribed into shaping social institutions to correspond to, or even promote, the values and structures of the dominating center of the system.
>
> (Schiller, 1976: 9)

In fact, this definition clearly shows how much Schiller was influenced by Immanuel Wallerstein's (1974) World System approach, as discussed earlier. He admits in the first lines of his book that cultural imperialism follows and combines Wallerstein's categorization of what composes the modern world system, even going one step further by identifying what those components are, including a single market; a set of government structures; and the appropriation of surplus labour. Consequently, cultural imperialism "develops in a world system within which there is a single market, and the terms and character of production are determined in the core of that market and radiate outward" (Ibid: 5).

Viewed in this manner, Schiller argued that the relationship between the core and peripheries in Wallerstein's model is certainly apparent and applicable when it comes to the structure and the flow of information and communication internationally. Since within the modern world economy, class structure and hegemony are the basis of the relationship between the core countries—the highly developed West—and the peripheries—the Third World or developing countries. Clearly, he believed that the process of economic penetration in the markets for gaining profits is similarly applicable in the field of communication, where giant media monopolies and cultural conglomerates possess the same objectives. He asserted that "the cultural penetration that has occurred in recent decades embraces all the socializing institutions of the affected host area" (Ibid: 8). Focusing on this point, Schiller argued that there are different patterns of cultural imperialism as a denial of the Right to Communicate cultures. The first is related to the content of cultural programming. For instance, a clear example of this conceptualization is the distribution of Disney comics in Third World countries, which started in the 1940s, and which has had a widespread impact on their cultures, showing the utilization of cultural materials as carriers of American capitalist values. Dorfman and Mattelart in their *How to Read Donald Duck: Imperialist Ideology in the Disney Comic* (1975), argued that:

> The Disney comics aren't really about small furry and feathery animals sent off by a comics uncle to have adventures searching for gold in fantasy lands called Inca-Blinca . . . they are about the capitalist-imperialist words-view implicit in the narrative.
>
> (cited in Tomlinson, 1991: 43)

In other words, American cultural imperialism exports cultural products that embody American capitalist values.[22] Secondly, on the educational level, Schiller criticized the character of educational and scientific institutions in the core as well as the way in which they lead the peripherals countries, which "are compelled to adapt to and serve the requirements of the multinational corporate economy" (Schiller, 1976: 11). In addition to these content patterns, cultural imperialism is also establishing a worldwide concentration by monopolizing the training of corporate managers, as well as in the education of journalists.[23]

The most pressing discourses of imperialism that affected the thoughts of Schiller, which are pertinent to this discussion, are the critiques of the discourses of American modernization and the World System approach. He articulated both Lerner's theory of communication and development and the United Nations Educational, Scientific and Cultural Organization (UNESCO) criteria for the "minimally desirable levels of media adequacy for development. These were the familiar ratios of newspaper consumption, radio sets, cinema seats, etc., per capita" (Ibid: 49). He then commented that the only way these facts could be explained or justified is through "imperialism." Furthermore, dependency theorists applied the Wallersteinian categorization to the global communication system[24] where the core countries (the North, West, and U.S.) dominate the flow of information to their former colonial countries (peripheries). Therefore, Schiller considered technology as the vehicle of cultural domination: "It is imperative today to consider the general role of technology not only as an instrument for effectuating cultural domination but as an embodiment of this very domination" (1976: 47).

Regardless of Schiller's contribution to the launching of a theory of cultural imperialism, it goes without saying that he came under a great deal of criticism.[25] Mosco argues that one critic believed Schiller was a "one-dimensional thinker, [and] an economic determinist who saw capitalism as an omnipotent singularity" (2001: 196). In spite of this, Mosco, asserts that they are "flat out wrong" (Ibid), and that it is true that he concentrated on the power of global capitalism, predominantly the power of the transnational media in the world (such as AOL Time/Warner, Disney, etc.), arguing that capitalism is a complex system and not merely a unilateral economic form. For this reason, Schiller was concerned, even in his earliest works, with the role of government, as well as of the military, as key players in the field of information, either advancing or opposing corporate power. Mosco adds, "it was possible to oppose the global media industry and to produce an alternative to commercial culture" (Ibid) since Schiller believes that culture is contingent to democracy. For this reason, his later works involved the examination of the cultural significance of different media in our lives (such as parks, streets, museums, etc.) which represent "for him . . .

'a community's economic life [which] cannot be separated from its symbolic contact' and that 'speech, dance, drama, music and the visual and plastic arts have been vital, indeed necessary, features of human experience from the earliest times'" (Ibid: 197).

Thus, what I have tried to cover here through the work of Herbert Schiller, is that he has employed the term "culture" as a way of life,[26] and did not merely limit it to the communication media, as many of his critics claimed. Inspired by his life experience and background, influenced by different streams of intellectual efforts (such as those of Fanon and Wallerstein), and believing in the people's right of cultural independence and self-determination, he elaborated an original contribution through his notion of "cultural imperialism" which certainly played a key role in many subsequent efforts. For example, the (NWICO) based its claims on Schiller's conception of the "have" and "have-not" regions; this concept is certainly one central tenet of the advancement of the Right to Communicate concept and communication rights' movement. Mosco, supporting Schiller's arguments, explains that even with the spread of the "utopian rhetoric" of the "wired democracy" evident during the new communication media boom (such as the Internet), Schiller confidently argued that both old and new media were "expanding the power of transitional media" (Mosco, 2001: 193).

My reading of Schiller presumes that for him, cultural imperialism is certainly not trade or commercial exchange; it is more a division between the core and the periphery countries. For that, cultural imperialism forms one plausible example of the theorization of the Right to Communicate concept. As for Schiller, this forms a violation of the Right to Communicate where the core countries send, not only the capitalists' commercial and economic productions, but also its political, cultural, and social values of individualism, freedom, and liberty as viewed and practiced by the West. Further, as seen in his work, it was squarely emphasized that this unequal exchange of communication may also include sending cultural productions, that are manufactured for the capitalist consumer, to non-Western consumers in order to gain greater profit and, in so doing, negatively affecting the culture, language, traditions, habits, norms, values, and life-styles of the Third World audience. These ideas are pertinent to further elaboration and theorization of the Right to Communicate concept as they are applying Dewey's conception of communication as a "social understanding" on the one hand, and Habermas' right-based communication model on the other where the sender of communicative message must meet the receiver's demands from him or her in order to engage with in communication. Undeniably, such ideals are not a part of the communicative patterns Schiller's discusses and criticizes in the preceding analysis of cultural imperialism.

Notes

1. Anderson and Major affirm that Dewey thinks human beings "have strong impulses toward compassion, justice, and equality, because he believes that humans have a sixth sense about fairness" (2001: 105). They add that if Dewey were to come back again and discover the violations of rights and "racism," he would be "disappointed."

2. Habermas admitted, "I have for a long time identified myself with that radical democratic mentality which is present in the best American traditions and articulated in American pragmatism" (Shalin, 1992: 238).

3. The main point that attracted Habermas to American pragmatist anchor Dewey's philosophy is "freedom of inquiry, toleration of diverse views, freedom of communication, the distribution of what is found out to every individual as the ultimate intellectual consumer, [and that these] are involved in the democratic as in the scientific method" (Shalin 1992: 246).

4. It is important to remember that neither the developing countries nor the Axis countries (Japan, Germany, and Italy) participated in the languaging of the *Universal Declaration of Human Rights* in 1948.

5. Particularly, he condemns this situation pinpointing that, "For me the North African interlude was a powerful prod to consciousness. What later came to be called . . . the Third World, the developing world, and, most recently, "emerging markets," continues to be . . . the part of the world where great numbers of people live and die under frightfully deprived conditions" (Schiller, 2000: 18).

6. It is interesting to mention here that Schiller's reputation as a new-comer to the field of communication studies during the 1960s led to his early work being dismissed by communication scholars of the time, which in turn led to his own personal route in the development of his intellectual life and future critical analysis. For instance, his interpretation of American imperialism in his first book was underestimated by such established American scholars as Daniel Lerner, who evaluated Schiller's position as "naïve" and treated Schiller as "a nobody." Lerner considered Schiller's work to be pro-communist, commenting that, "it is difficult to assess the influence of the New Left on communication. It contributed nothing to research; where it bothered at all with data, these were collected by conventional methods never going beyond rudimentary content analysis. It contributed nothing to theory" (1980: 137). According to Schiller, however, it was advantageous to be a "nobody" for a while, as it gave him the opportunity to thoroughly investigate the global research on communication powers far from the spotlight that would be trained on a more established scholar, until he produced "a body of material that finally could not be ignored" (cited in Maxwell, 2003: 26).

7. For example, he published many essays and articles in newspapers and magazines, such as *The Nation*, *The Progressive*, and the *Administrative Law Review*, among others. Maxwell says that in 1968, Schiller combined many of these articles into his first book (2003: 25–26).

8. For example, he hoped that the pioneering efforts by some Third World's "heroes" such as Nehru in India, Sukarno in Indonesia, Tito in Yugoslavia, Castro in Cuba, Abdel-Nasser in Egypt, and Nkrumah in Ghana, among others, would succeed, (Maxwell, 2003: 24–25).

9. See Immanuel Wallerstein in his "The Rise and Future Demise of the World Capitalist System: Concepts for Comparative Analysis" (1974), and his "Semi-Peripheral Countries and the Contemporary World Crisis" (1976), in which he argues that the World Economy became a fixed model as early as the 1640s because this is where unequal exchange between the core-periphery countries first becomes evident, not only in terms of economic factors but also in power relations.

10. Schiller continued to support his assertion by arguing that the U.S. military efforts clearly controlled the fate of communication technologies by promoting the capitalist system during the development of these media. Taking radio for example, he says that the U.S. government urged this medium to adopt the rules of equipment manufacturers first, then pushed it "into the arms" of the advertising-based business (Schiller, 1969: 69).

11. Such as Daniel Kruger, who attacked Schiller, among other scholars who he believed to be pro-communist since they generally opposed the American expansion of the capitalist system. Given this article's time frame, one should mention here that Kruger's opinion might represent a belief that coincided with the cold-war period in the U.S., where intellectual positions opposing capitalism

were suspected of being communist. Therefore, he believed that to combine imperialism and American capitalism is not accurate or fair: "it is certainly misleading to describe by the same word 'imperialism' both the European statesmen who plan ruthlessly to overrun a country in Asia or Africa and the American company building an automobile assembly plant in Israel" (Kruger, 1955: 252).

12. John Atkinson Hobson (1858–1940) is among the first scholars who studied the term imperialism. He particularly argued that imperialism is not merely a political or territorial expansion of one power over new colonies. Instead, it embodies other dimensions (since it aims to establish political control primarily for economic purposes), and seeks to justify itself through ethical and humanitarian reasons. Further, he explained that a scientific defence of imperialism is built on a natural selection argument, in which the Englishman "believes he is a more excellent type than any other man; he believes that he is better able to assimilate any special virtues others may have; he believes that this character gives him a right to rule which no other can possess" (1902: 465). In this respect, Hobson added that the main motive behind the idea of imperialism in Western thinking during the early twentieth century, especially in Europe, was that maintaining a level of struggle between races and types of civilization is positive and even beneficial. Indeed, this kind of struggle is considered as "the chief moral support of imperialism" (Ibid: 462).

13. Scholars argue that cultural imperialism can be perceived as a discourse of nationality in which claims for the need to maintain national culture against foreign cultural domination are the central idea, especially in the developing countries. Here, the assumption adopted is that the collective shared values and traditions of a nation-state are threatened by an outside power(s). In fact, there are two limitations to this view: the first is to believe that there are

monolithic shared values among the people living within particular boundaries; patterns of cultural identification may be different across (and within) national boundaries. However, the nation-state is regarded as the only "political-economic unit into which the world is divided" (Tomlinson, 1991: 69) which is responsible for both ideological and cultural construction. The second problem arises from considering space as the only unit of analysis, thus either ignoring the time factor altogether, or considering it as "frozen" (Ibid). Thus, cultural imperialism as a discourse of nationality emphasizes the geographical—or spatial—culture, while making the assumption that they do not change through time, an idea that makes no sense in the face of the communication media and their impact on developing, and combining different spatial cultures. One of the most obvious examples of cultural identity as a discourse of nationality can be seen in the some of the contributions in the NWICO debate, articulated by the MacBride Commission.

14. Despite his short life, Frantz Fanon (1925–1961) is considered as one of the most influential figures in the anti-colonialism movement of the 1950s. According to Gordon et al, Fanon's work had a great impact on political theory research, post-modern cultural writings and post-colonial studies, such as is found in the works of Edward Said and Homi Bhabha. The authors add that Fanon's writing and advocacy for equality and egalitarianism was attacked by those of diverging political positions like the anti-black, anti-Caribbean, and anti-Arab (1996: 5–6) groups. In his first essay, *Peau Noire, Masques Blancs* (1952), he accurately portrayed the impact of colonization's imposed techniques on the life-styles of the people using different media of communication. One technique was to alienate the people by penetrating into their life through the use of books, schools, films, and radio among other media, to persuade them to only one

point of view: the white—or European perspective. An interesting and plausible explanation of the way colonial administrations combine imperialism and culture is the case of Algerian society under French colonization. In his *A Dying Colonialism* (1965), Fanon explained that Algerian opposition confronted French efforts to annihilate Algerian culture by trying to "unveil" Algerian women. Imperialist powers understood the significance and high esteem of the female location in this culture, and for this reason, believed that "it was the woman who was given the historic mission of shaking up the Algerian man" (1965: 38). In other words, destroying Algerian culture starts with "Westernizing" Algerian women, planting the Western seeds within the Algerian soil, and then, when it is enriched and grown, it will arguably transform the social culture into a Western format. Within the broad spectrum of racist practices used by colonial imperialists during the post-World War Two era in the developing and Third World countries, Schmitt says that for Fanon, imperialist forces: 1) infantilize the dependent nations and treat them as children; 2) denigrate and stereotype the subject groups, from the assumption that they are defective; 3) constantly distrust members of the subject group even if they are skillful; 4) mock and underestimate them; and 5) treat those excluded as invisible, where the only existing universal culture is the Western and white culture (1996: 37–38).

15. Here, Schiller (1976: 123) gives an example of the case of early broadcasting in Canada where many Canadians felt what was disseminated through the airwaves coming from their southern borders was not representing their own culture(s), tastes, or needs. Schiller cited one example of early Canadian efforts to confront American imperialism in this field: Henry Comor's 1967 report *American TV: What have you done to us?* in which he argued that American television is threatening Canadian national identity.

16. Mowlana adds that Schiller's writings came at the height of American dominance, and during the Third World's struggle to challenge American power and policies, particularly in the post-colonial period. Furthermore, he maintains that Schiller's spirit and the power of his beliefs have inspired many intellectuals and scholars in the developing countries, in particular, in Asia and Latin America (Mowlana, 2001: 21–23).

17. Particularly, he says that "What was so crucial about Herb's work at this time was that while many of us were thinking along the same lines, he was the one taking major steps to articulate and put it before the wider audiences of both students and faculty, not only in the United States but also in Europe and elsewhere" (Mowlana, 2001: 21).

18. I agree with Merrill in using "communication imperialism" terminology since this term incorporates both media and cultural imperialism.

19. Dennis, in support of this idea, argued "the reasons for the dominance of American content are obvious. We produce more programming and make it available more economically than any other nation in the world. Naturally, we are the primary supplier" (Dennis, 1984: 184).

20. Merrill gives many examples of the Third World's media practitioners, and opinion leaders' responsibility in imperialism claims. He says that in many conferences, he has met Third World journalists and editors who express their opposition to American and Western sensationalistic coverage of their news. After these conferences have ended, however, he has accompanied them to their offices where he witnessed that they selectively chose what is and what is not published. "I have accompanied them to their newspaper office. What did I find there? They themselves were choosing and playing up the non-serious, sensational news items, throwing the

serious stories into the waste basket (and there were plenty of important stories . . . Is this *imperialism* on the part of the West? I think not" (1984: 180).

21. Schiller was particularly impressed with the Chilean attempts to build an "anti-Western" communication system, which he, along with other scholars (such as Armand Mattelart) worked for the Chilean President Salvadore Allende on a "national communication policy" (Mosco, 2001: 194–195).

22. It is interesting to mention here that Mattelart expanded this analysis to include not only American comics but also American children's educational programs such as the famous *Sesame Street* that is distributed all over the world and translated into several languages (see Tomlinson, 1991: 65). In many places around the world, the American *Sesame Street* is considered to be a hallmark in the children programming. For many, watching *Sesame Street* means consuming American culture, which is ironically not seen to be negative at all to them; to the contrary, it is a symbol of elitism and a high standard of living.

23. In this regard, Schiller documented the fact that major American universities are establishing educational centers outside the U.S., especially in the developing countries (1976: 11–12).

24. Tomlinson comments on this point saying that "However, it must be said that Schiller tends to present a fairly simple version which glosses over some of the tricky conceptual problems involved and in which the notion of 'the system' becomes reified and operates in a rather crude and rigid 'functionalist' manner" (Tomlinson, 1991: 38).

25. Outlining the differing criticisms of many researchers towards Schiller's theorizing of cultural imperialism, Tomlinson argues that Schiller has rightly been criticized for this functionalism, since he linked cultural imperialism to capitalism, arguing that developed capitalist

countries use their cultural products to attract developing countries' cultures in order to expand their capitalist audience. In other words, Schiller's account of cultural imperialism relies too much on the structure of media institutions and their function as tools for the promotion of American imperialism to the extent that, and I would agree, that he appears to be advocating for a media imperialism discourse and not for one of cultural imperialism. However, Tomlinson adds that despite this criticism, Schiller's analysis is not simply "a view of cultural imperialism as recruiting sergeant for the capitalist economic order" (1991: 104). Rather he believed that the capitalist world system embodies within itself a deterministic vision of the necessary prerequisites for global cultural development. Further, the analysis of Schiller was much admired by McPhail, where he argues that "Some critics, such as Schiller, have probed perhaps even more deeply into the "who communicates" question and have found that the real source, the real shaper, of Third World communication systems and the messages they produce is the West" (1981: 77).

26. Tomlinson added that Schiller was inspired by the critical perspective of the Frankfurt School and those who heavily criticized capitalist powers. He adds that "This is seen as shaping the way things are at all levels of Western societies, from the military-industrial complex to the personal-existential experience of citizen-consumers" (Tomlinson, 1991: 39).

Chapter 6

The Question of the Right to Communicate

In reviewing the preceding discussions of the history of thought regarding "rights" in general, and the "communication right" in particular, one could conclude that there are three distinct historical dimensions to the question of treating communication as a "right." The first is the formal languaging of this right in various declarations and covenants. Next, it must be considered whether there is any such right in real life, and if so, what are its justifications and the possible limits. Finally is the attempt to realize the "right" to communicate, however understood, in actual practices.

The Language Answer

The creation of an international language of human rights is an important dimension that crowns the recognition of the "right" to communicate as one of the basic human rights. The formal, legal, positive, and protective language of human rights functions to both protect human beings against violations of their rights and to conjoin individuals and states in practicing these rights. As previously outlined, there is more than one historical declaration that could be considered as the first seeds of languaging the Right to Communicate, such as those that arose from the American and French revolutions.

Despite their importance in this historical exploration, they are still not considered "universal" as they uphold and protect this right, among others, only for their respective national citizens. The *Universal Declaration of Human Rights* in 1948 was the first "universal" language of these rights and provided a legal document for the enforcement of the Right to Communicate, not only on the individual level, but also in the social and international realm. This document was the spark that brought about several covenants, conferences, treatises and declarations to reinforce the historic development thereafter.

As a result of this formal language, a shift occurred in the growth of the Right to Communicate. Before these different languages, the Right to Communicate was simply an individual freedom, that is, an entitlement at the time and place a claim was made that lacked the guarantee that it could be claimed or accepted at all times or by everyone. Following this phase, the Right to Communicate started to be considered a "right," at least in language as seen for example in the *International Covenant on Civil and Political Rights* (1966), and the *International Covenant on Economic, Social and Cultural Rights* (1966), among other legal declarations, documents, and covenants.

The Realization Phase

The realization dimension was crucial as it paved the way for the recognition of the importance of this right for humanity. Initially, the conception of the Right to Communicate was rooted in philosophy; it was an understanding articulated by various intellectuals, thinkers, and philosophers who began to realize how important communication is for human beings. They voiced their support for the high degree of enjoyment of these freedoms without constraints imposed by authorities like governments and churches. These freedoms were eventually guaranteed to citizens for the first time in the declarations that arose out of the American and French Revolutions. They also expressed the nature of these freedoms on a moral level, believing that although they are absolute, people must channel them for good purposes.

A final characteristic of this dimension, which could be considered an obstacle in the history of the Right to Communicate, is the emphasis on the individual, in human rights in general, and the Right to Communicate in particular. As there are no boundaries for the Right to Communicate, the main concern was to emancipate the individual from constraints and oppression, without special attention or regard for other individuals or the rest of society.

Milton, in seventeenth century England, realized the significance of communication and its two inseparable aspects: that individuals should enjoy a high degree of freedom to express and access information and communication, while at the same time acknowledging a moral and religious responsibility to use it for good purposes. Coupled with his emphasis on freedom of thought, expression, and the press, and his refusal to accept any kind of pre-censorship to limit or suppress the expression of this freedom, Milton believed in the essential goodness of human nature. The individual would make good use of these freedoms by making good choices.

Moreover, as clarified previously, Milton was defending only one dimension of the Right to Communicate—the pre-publication dimension—as he allows for post-censorship that confines, or burns, "bad" books. Would Milton still defend this position in contemporary society? Would he still advocate the right of human beings to communicate through publishing, authorship, the press, and other media on the basis of his belief in the human capability to make good and moral choices, in keeping with "Christian values"? Similarly, Voltaire could be asked the following whether he would still demand tolerance, even for those who engage in hate speech in the Internet? Would Mill still use the claim of absolute liberty and free speech to defend the publishing of pornography? The answers to these questions are crucial.

Although these philosophers advocated an absolute Right to Communicate, and contributed greatly to our contemporary recognition of the concepts of freedom, justice, and morality, relying solely on their positions as the basis of a possible Right to Communicate, is clearly insufficient. It has been made clear that both language and philosophical realization need an "enforcement" or a "practice" dimension to determine the basic characteristics of potential communication rights that can be backed by universal language and receive the acceptance of all human beings and societies.

The Practice Debate

The theory, formalization in language, and realization of the Right to Communicate have built the foundation for moving forward, but in attempting to link words and practice, contradictions become evident. While the language makes a universal Right to Communicate available for all human beings without any distinction, practicing this right creates possible conflicts: the existing social and political systems and circumstances and one's own right as opposed to the practice of the same right by others. Chapter 3 extensively illustrated the latter case by showing where problems and difficulties exist when the Right to Communicate is practiced in an absolute and universal way.

Given their history, human rights, from their emergence (before the language of the *Universal Declaration of Human Rights'*) to the present, are still not universal in practice. The *First Amendment* of the American *Declaration of Independence*, for instance, guaranteed universal equal rights for all human beings but excluded slaves from entitlement to these rights, even though both slaves and other Americans were living in the same place at the same time. Moreover, in recent years, despite all international efforts, human beings continue to suffer from violations of their rights, from social, physical, economic, and educational rights in general, and to communication rights in particular. Many international, national, regional, and local bodies have documented violations in numerous countries every year. In fact, this particular claim is one of the bases of the relativity approach to human rights.

If humans are treated as sacred, then how can violations of this kind be justified? In the Rwandan and Bosnian massacres, for example, many human rights were violated. In the context of communication, rights are violated in the mass media when entities, such as the giant conglomerate media, interfere in journalists' editorials because they own the newspapers. Do they realize that they are violating the journalists' right to communicate their ideas? Or do they believe that journalists only have a right to communicate the ideas of their media owners?

Concerning the historical development of this issue, the contributions of medieval and eighteenth century philosophy are rich in conceiving the main principles of the Right to Communicate. At the same time, however, they fail to offer a comprehensive guideline or provide solutions for the current controversies between the ideal universal language of the Right to Communicate and its practice. Alternatively, the contemporary philosophies of Dewey and Habermas, as presented in Chapter 5, offer part of a possible solution for the universality argument by clarifying whether communication could be considered a basic human right or not. Together, Dewey and Habermas offer a clear-cut understanding of the absolute Right to Communicate.

Dewey conceptualized communication as a "social conversation" between individuals living in society, where it is necessary to exercise freedom of expression, speech, and democracy. Therefore, he would reject the claims of absolute practice of those in society who would claim for a right to communication without allowing participants to exchange their messages equally, as in the case of propaganda.

For his part, Habermas outlines prerequisites for the *Ideal Speech Situation* and validity claims for communicative action. He articulates that any human speech should maintain the validity claims: to be truthful, justified, true, and sincere in order to claim its universalistic nature. Yet, although fruitfully informing us about the ethics of communication, one can see that this is a seemingly utopian ideal and is hardly adoptable in many real life circumstances by different actors in the international communication sphere (such as the many voices that criticized the NWICO debate and the universal Right to Communicate). The work of Herbert Schiller is one possible example of theorizing the Right to Communicate concept. Particularly through his study of the Right to Communicate within the different power relations that exist in real life (be it political, social, economical, and cultural), and attempting to suggest that a threat to the human exercise of one's own language, opinions, thoughts, norms, values, cultures, and information, is a violation of a Right to Communicate.

The history of this issue has brought the debate to this point, where another element of the argument arises. In the context of analyzing the Right to Communicate in our contemporary, globalized and digital society, the following question must be examined: What would be more important for humans in discussing their Right to Communicate: language or practice? Or, put another way; is the possession of the right in language more important than its social practice? Answering this question is complex, especially in the context of recent years with the rise of new and modern communication technologies, and within the intertwinement of the different power relations in our contemporary societies.

At the core of this discussion is the fact that, given the universal language of the Right to Communicate, the practice of this right is evidently not universal; instead, it is ironically leaning towards being an authoritative type of communication in society. In other words, the more modern or civilized a society becomes, the more power is given to authority to control communication media. In fact, d'Arcy predicted this evolution during the 1960s when he argued that it was not so long ago that human beings were able to communicate freely with each other by seeing and listening. Subsequently, as they increasingly became dependent on technology as the medium to communicate, they have alienated themselves from each other:

> In point of fact, it is not yet one hundred years since man has been able to hear over a distance, and barely forty since he has been able to see beyond the horizon. The achievement dazzled him, and the extraordinarily complex organization, public or private, that was set up forced him to accept a restriction of freedom that he had previously rejected for other vehicles of thought.
>
> (d'Arcy, 1977: 2)

Accordingly, this point leads to a further investigation of the meaning of "communication" and a discussion of whether it could be treated as a human right, fundamental to existence in a democratic society. Defining communication has not been an easy task for scholars and researchers for several reasons, one of which is its normative nature. Scholars and theorists in this field have contributed hundreds of definitions of communication, and some have concluded that "the verb 'to communicate' is well established in the common lexicon and therefore is not easily captured for scientific use. Indeed, it is one of the most overworked terms in the English language" (Littlejohn, 2002: 6). Communication is conceived according to Gunnar Naesselund, the former UNESCO Director of the Department of Free Flow of Information and Development, as the following:

> [Communication] is not an end in itself, but rather a wide-ranging set of means by which human beings and their social institutions can discuss,

> react and take steps towards goals defined by themselves. It is an element of life—an attitude and a demonstration of a basic faith in the potential of human beings.
>
> (Fisher, 1982: 11)

Realistically, communication plays a vital and pervasive role in our lives, and d'Arcy, for one, asserts this importance in all societies: "All social organization rests upon communication among its constituent parts. All beings are dependent upon communication with their kind. All social organization results from communication," adding that "Indeed all social structure rests upon and evolves within the framework of those methods of communication available to it at any given time" (1977: 46).

Before beginning to address the core question of this book, it is useful to first move away from the abstract debate surrounding this issue and attempt to understand some examples of the practice of communication as a human right, however it is realized.

Perspectives on the Right to Communicate

The example below is presented mainly to illustrate how the Right to Communicate is treated normatively in practice or in real life. In her report, *The Right to Communicate: A Socialist Approach*, a key paper in the MacBride Commission Report, Jadwiga Pastecka states that

> The right to communicate is a natural human right but at the same time it is a social phenomenon strongly shaped and defined by the socio-economic conditions, ideological assumptions and cultural values of a given country . . . the right to communi-

cate is a product of social structure, because, . . . it is not the way people communicate that determines the social structures it is the social structures that determine the way people communicate.

(Pastecka, 1982: 1)

This perspective asserts that information is a basic human element necessary in social communication but only when it is practiced in a manner that adheres to a "socialist" society's ideology. Pastecka goes on to argue that:

The socialist concept of communication system is devised to give the people some general picture of the world or at least of its most important problems, it treats information and news as elements of certain logical, complex, coherent, and rational knowledge in all important fields of life both local and international which is necessary to a modern man for a full individual life and social functioning in the contemporary world.

(Ibid: 2–3)

One can see the vast difference between this concept of communication and the Deweyian notion that recognizes communication as "social thinking" between individuals that is not imposed by authorities or laws that identify and regulate it. Is that not what Schiller refuted in his criticism of imposing a particular social, cultural, and political structure in societies without a free input from the public themselves?

In this example, the practice of the Right to Communicate is bound by certain rules that are convenient to this society and are prescribed either by the authorities of the system or the major powers in society. Hence, the socialist prerequisite for the Right to Communicate is that it should preferably be consistent with the perspectives and judgments of those in positions of authority. Accordingly, the role of authorities is to control the flow of information in order to filter out "distorted," "false," and "inaccurate" types of communication. Pastecka continues:

> One is ready to admit that although this system of communication is psychologically healthy and socially sound it is not so attractive as its competitor: the news about the opening of a new nursery has a poor chance of attracting attention in comparison with the news about a madman who killed 7 nurses during one night!
>
> (Ibid)

Critically, could this model of communication possibly embody an understanding of a balanced Right to Communicate rather than an authority that disseminates information? Contradicting this position, Habermas offers an alternative perspective that requires the individuals society to participate in free communicative discourse in order to agree upon a given social accepted value:

> In justifying the system of rights, . . . the only legitimate law is one that emerges from the discursive opinion-and will-formation of equally enfranchised citizens. The latter can in turn adequately exercise their public autonomy, guaranteed by rights of communication and participation, only insofar as their private autonomy is guaranteed.
>
> (Habermas, 1998: 408)

In short, the Right to Communicate was, and still is, a "vague" concept for many people and systems, backed by a universal language, but needs to be a real illustration of the societies' own practice of these catchy concepts of "freedom," "equality," and "rights" among humans and not only what authorities disseminate.

It is interesting and pertinent to analyze some other practices of the Right to Communicate in recent times, especially in comparison with the previous example. The practice of journalism is an appropriate starting point. The primary component in a journalist's message is his or her "accuracy" in gathering and interpreting news stories and opinions. This is a qualification that can be seen, to a great extent, in the language of the Habermasian validity claims, namely "truth," "sincere," "justified," and "comprehensible." If the journalist deceives his or her readers or manipulates them with "false" and "undistorted" news stories, he or she will lose credibility and, consequently, readership. Although Habermas has been criticized for his "ideal" perspective concerning the role of validity claims in real life, it can be argued that to convey a message such as a news story, a journalist must meet the demands of his or her readers as the recipients of the message.

Consider Letters to Editors where anyone can express his or her opinion concerning a policy, an issue, or a problem, as one instance of the Right to Communicate in practice. At the same time, if this letter is criticizing someone, this person has the right to respond in the same place the criticism was published. Cartooning and editorials, along with several others forms of communication patterns, are examples of the actual realization of the Right to Communicate in practice. Briefly, journalism ethics are an important element, and an evident example in recent times, as they embody both public's right to information and the obligation of journalists, news agencies, and communication institutions to their audience.

Controversial, and therefore more complex, examples of the Right to Communicate in practice are the publishing of adult materials and the broadcasting of adult programs. Although this type of message is arguably not considered "communication," it is practiced differently in real life. Considering that people are exercising their "freedom" to access adult materials, it is implied that they should remain within the regulations and laws of society. In practical terms, if anyone wants to air an adult advertisement, he or she should first attach classification (i.e. rating) labels so that those under 18 years of age, along with other "receivers" that should not, or do not wish to come by these messages, are not exposed to them. In other words, their right is bound by moral and legal responsibility toward others to respect and ensure that they do not violate their privacy and their right "not" to receive these types of messages.

Is Communication a Basic Human Right?

Synthesizing the previously discussed theoretical frameworks and the multitude of arguments regarding the treatment of the Right to Communicate, one is left with the following fundamental question: Is communication a basic human right or not?

A single answer to this question cannot be provided, so instead, a possible position is offered. Given the different philosophical positions and intellectual contributions that came about in the historical exploration of this issue from the seventeenth century onward, it can be argued that setting guidelines might be the key determinant for answering this question, and thus widely understanding the Right to Communicate and its nature.

Firstly, the meaning of a "right" is required: a right is absolute when it is valid without reservation of any kind. Accordingly, it is admitted that there are no absolute rights, as even the very fundamental rights, such as the right to life, are not considered absolute. Sometimes, rights can be violated, either with justification—such as cases and circumstances of war, and situations of self-defense, for example—or without justification—like murder or terrorism. Therefore, the same is applicable to communication. Instead, recalling the Hohfeldian correlative relationship, it is found that the plausible standpoint is to regard communication as a right, but one that is bound by a certain degree of "duty" or "responsibility" toward others. If the right to communicate ideas, thoughts, opinions, etc., is claimed by someone, that person should be, at the same time, under both moral and legal "responsibility" to meet the social and ethical demands of recipients of his or her messages.

Secondly, the level of communication is required: communication could be considered as a basic human right according to its level. Advocates for the absolute Right to Communicate are correct in their argument that no one can deny there is a level of communication that is considered absolute, universal, and non-negotiable. A human being is a social animal, and in order to live, he or she must communicate. Jean d'Arcy maintains that "man has a specific, biological, need to communicate" (1982: 2), and even in applying his argument on the social plane, the same concept is still observed: "Communities, to coexist, require to communicate between themselves" (Fisher, 1982: 7), which is to a great extent similar to Dewey's conceptualization of the role of communication in society.

Interestingly, this position has broadened the notion of "communication" to include different levels, starting from the conscious, inter-personal, personal (face-to-face), inter-group, and mass communication. Different formats of communication are also delineated, ranging from signs, expressions, and words—as patterns of verbal communication—to gestures, body and paralanguage communication.

Based on the previous discussion, one can see that the level of communication is an important parameter in answering the primary questions of this book. Communication that is necessary for human existence is a basic human right. No one can deny that even prisoners are allowed to see other prisoners, or have a visit permit to see their relatives, although they should not be allowed to have a phone in their cells.

Thirdly, the content and usage of communication is required: a final guideline to answer the previous question is related to the content and use of communication. Many communication practices claim for legal and social enforcement though the content of these practices could never be considered as "communication." Hate speech, harming people with offensive language or using signs and communication to manipulate people can never be considered, as a basic human right. One can list a variety of reasons not to accept these "messages," among them are morals, ethics, and social values. Instead the Habermasian validity claims can simply be used as a guide for communicative action that leads to "understanding" between human beings, and societies.

Considering Marshall McLuhan's famous statement, "the medium is the message"—which implies that medium and message are the two basic components of the communication process—signals that, in the context of this discussion, the recent language of rights has obviously covered a variety of message formats and different media. Formats vary from "holding," "seeking," "receiving," "imparting," and "expressing" information, as a right for everyone through any kind of media, without any frontiers or barriers.

Consequently, given the continuous advancements of modern technologies in the field of communication and information, it has admittedly been difficult in recent years to define and elaborate a single position on the Right to Communicate that can be generalized over time, as well as be accepted by all cultures and ideologies around the world. It is clear that if scholars had defined this right a decade ago, the definition would not be applicable today. Television, as a medium, is different from Direct Broadcast Satellite (DBS), and newspapers are different from the Internet. Collectively, the concept of the Right to Communicate needs continuous and further elaboration. Jean d'Arcy outlines in the 1960s that, the Right to Communicate concept is "as yet inchoate concept, a concept of the future, still in the making" (1982: 1).

Finally, as communication scholars, we must work toward defining and finding a way to realize the importance of communication as a basic human right. Until now, communication rights remain in abstract language and must still be practiced in a way that fits into every culture and society. The possible solution proposed in this book, deriving from the positions of both Dewey and Habermas, is first to assert communication as a social conversation in society that stems from its social facts and environment, and is capable, at the same time, to produce its own normative rules and to practice the value of communication in an acceptable form for everyone in society. One of these important norms is democracy, where every member in society is practicing communication in different ways: politically, socially, culturally, etc.

The mass media are one of the key players in raising public awareness of the importance of the Right to Communicate as a social value and, at the same time, a channel in which to exercise it. In the context of ethics, communication should be an intelligible, comprehensible, justified, sincere, and pure process, as proposed by Habermas, in order to be acceptable in society. Nevertheless, the Right to Communicate must acquire a more powerful position, derived from the practice and enforcement of the strong language that housed in the various national and international declarations.

References

Ali, Shaheen Sardar. (2000). *Gender and human rights in Islam and international law: Equal before Allah, unequal before man?* Boston: Kluwer Law International.

Allen, R. E. (1987). The speech of Glaucon: On contract the common good. In Spiro Panagiotou (Ed.), *Justice, law and method in Plato and Aristotle* (pp. 51–62). Edmonton: Academic Printing & Publishing.

Amin, Samir. (1976). *Unequal development: An essay on the social formations of peripheral capitalism* (Brian Pearce, Trans.). Hassocks: Harvester Press.

Amin, Samir. (1977). Imperialism and unequal development. New York: Monthly Review Press.

Anderson, Debra J. & Major, Robert L. (2001). Dewey, democracy, and citizenship. *Clearing House, 75*(2), 104–07.

Antonio, Robert J. (1989). The normative foundations of emancipatory theory: Evolutionary versus pragmatic perspectives. *American Journal of Sociology, 94*(4), 721–48.

Baehr, Peter R. (1999). *Human rights: Universality in practice.* New York: St. Martin's Press.

Baker, Keith Michael. (2001). On the Problem of the Ideological Origins of the French Revolution. In Ronald Schechter (Ed.), *The French revolution* (pp. 52–74). Malden: Blackwell Publishers Ltd.

Barron, Jerome A. & Dienes, Thomas C. (1979). *Handbook of free speech and free press.* Boston: Little, Brown and Company.

Bentham, Jeremy. (1987). An introduction to the principles of morals and legislation. In Alan Ryan (Ed.), *John Stuart Mill and Jeremy Bentham: Utilitarianism and other essays* (pp. 65–111). London: Penguin Books.

Bernier, Olivier. (1983). *Lafayette: Hero of two worlds*. New York: E.P. Dutton.

Bordas, Eric. (2003). The violence of tolerance: An aspect of Voltaire's rhetoric in the *Traité sur la tolérance* (1763). *South Central Review, 19/20*(4/1), 14–28.

Boylan, James. (1970). [Review of the book *mass communication and American empire*]. *Public Opinion Quarterly, 34*(3), 510–511.

Bradley, A. W. (2001). Magna Carta and the protection of human rights in Europe: The challenge of the 21st century. *Law and justice, 146*, 5–27.

Breckheimer, P. J. (2002). A haven for hate: The foreign and domestic implications of protecting Internet hate speech under the First Amendment. *Southern California Law Review, 75*(6), 1493–1528.

Brems, Eva. (2001). *Human rights: Universality and diversity*. The Hague: Martinus Nijhoff Publishers.

Canada. Department of Communications. Telecommission Studies. (1971). *Instant world: A report on telecommunications in Canada*. Ottawa: Information Canada.

Canada. House of Commons. (April 1997). Privacy: Where do we draw the line. Report of the House of Commons Standing Committee on Human Rights and the Status of Persons With Disabilities. Ottawa: Government Services.

Chartier, Roger. (2001). The cultural origins of the French revolution. In Ronald Schechter (Ed.), *The French revolution* (pp. 75–105). Malden: Blackwell Publishers Ltd.

Chase, Bob. (1997). John Locke and cultural relativism. *Interpretation, 25*(1), 59–90.

Cocca, Aldo Armando. (1982). The Right to Communicate: Some reflections on its legal foundation. In MacBride Commission Papers of International Communications, Collection Zimmerman, CBC/Radio-Canada. Institut International De La Communication: UNESCO.

Creppell, Ingrid. (1996). Locke on toleration: The transformation of constraint. *Political Theory*, 24(2), 200–40.

Cutler, Fred. (1999). Jeremy Bentham and the public opinion tribunal. *Public Opinion Quarterly*, 63(3), 321–46.

d'Arcy, Jean. (1969). Direct broadcast satellites and the Right to Communicate. *European Broadcasting Union Review*, 118, 14–18.

d'Arcy, Jean. (1977). The Right of Man to Communicate. In L. S. Harms, Jim Richstad, and Kathleen A. Kie (Eds.), *Right to Communicate: Collected papers* (pp. 45–52). Hawaii: The University Press of Hawaii.

d'Arcy, Jean. (1982). The Right to Communicate. In MacBride Commission Papers of International Communications, Collection Zimmerman, CBC/Radio-Canada. Institut International De La Communication: UNESCO.

Dakroury, Aliaa. (2005). Who owns the medium owns the message? The ambiguity of the Right to Communicate in the age of convergence. *Reconstruction: Studies in Contemporary Culture*, 5(2).

Dakroury, Aliaa. (2006). Anti- and counter-terrorism: Snagging the practice of a human Right to Communicate. In *Information-MFCSIT'06* (pp. 35–38). Cork, Ireland: National University of Ireland.

Dakroury, Aliaa. (2006, November 4). A right to insult?! The Danish cartoons controversy and the Right to Communicate in Islam. The 2nd Canadian conference of the Association of Muslim Social Scientists (AMSS)-Canada. Islam: Tradition and Modernity. Organized by The Association of Muslim Social Scientists (AMSS)-Canada and The Department of Near and Middle Eastern Civilizations. Toronto, University of Toronto.

Dakroury, Aliaa. (2008). *Present at the creation: Telecommission Studies and the intellectual origins of the Right to Communicate in Canada (1969–71)*. Unpublished doctoral dissertation, School of Journalism and Communication, Carleton University, Ottawa.

Darnton, Robert. (2001). The Forbidden Best-Sellers of the Pre-Revolutionary France. In Ronald Schechter (Ed.), *The French Revolution*. pp. 106–137. Malden: Blackwell Publishers Ltd.

Dennis, Everette E. & Merrill, John C. (1984). *Basic issues in mass communication: A debate*. New York: Macmillan.

Dewey, John. (1916). *Democracy and education: An introduction to the philosophy of education*. New York: The Free Press. [Reprinted 1966].

Dewey, John. (1935). *Liberalism and social action*. New York: Capricorn Books. [Reprinted 1963].

Dewey, John. (1939). *Freedom and culture*. New York: Capricorn Books. [Reprinted 1963].

Donnelly, Jack. (1999). The social construction of international human rights. In Tim Dunne and Nicholas Wheeler (Eds.), *Human rights in global politics* (pp. 71–102). UK: Cambridge University Press.

Dorfman, Ariel & Mattelart, Armand. (1991). How to read Donald Duck: Imperialist ideology in the Disney comic. New York: International General.

Douzinas, Costas. (2000). *The end of human rights: Critical legal thought at the turn of the century*. Oxford: Hart Publishing.

Fairchilds, Cissie. (2000). Fashion and freedom in the French revolution. *Continuity and Change, 15*(3), 419–33.

Feinberg, Joel. (1979). The nature and value of rights. In David Lyons (Ed.), *Rights* (pp. 78–91). Belmont: Wadsworth Publishing Company, Inc.

Fireman, Peter. (1957). *Justice in Plato's Republic*. New York: Philosophical Library.

Fisher, Desmond. (1982). The Right to Communicate: Towards a definition. In MacBride Commission Papers of International Communications, Collection Zimmerman, CBC/Radio-Canada. Institut International De La Communication: UNESCO.

Fisher, John. (1966). Plato on writing and doing philosophy. *Journal of the History of Ideas, 27*(2), 163–172.

Freeman, Michael. (1994). The philosophical foundations of human rights. *Human Rights Quarterly, 16*(3), 491–514.

Froman, Creel. (1992). *Language and power: Books I and II.* New Jersey: Humanities Press.

Furet, François. (1998). Democracy and utopia. *Journal of Democracy, 9*(1). 65–79.

Garnham, Nicholas. (2000). *Emancipation, the media and modernity: Arguments about the media and social theory.* Oxford: Oxford University Press.

Geuss, Raymond. (2001). *History and illusion in politics.* Cambridge: Cambridge University Press.

Gewirth, Alan. (1984). Are there any absolute rights? In Jeremy Waldron (Ed.), *Theories of rights* (pp. 91–109). New York: Oxford University Press.

Giddens, Anthony. (1985). Jürgen Habermas. In Quentin Skinner (Ed.), *The return of grand theory in the human sciences* (pp. 121–140). Cambridge: Cambridge University Press.

Gill, Emily R. (2001). Autonomy, diversity and the right to culture. In M. Leiser and Tom D. Campbell (Eds.), *Human rights in philosophy and practice* (pp. 285–302). Aldershot: Ashgate Darmouth.

Glendon, Mary Ann. (2001). *A world made new: Eleanor Roosevelt and the Universal Declaration of Human Rights.* New York: Random House.

Gray, John. (1988). Mill's and other liberalisms. In Knud Haakonssen (Ed.), *Traditions of liberalism: Essays on John Locke, Adam Smith and John Stuart Mill* (pp. 119–144). Australia: The Centre for Independent Studies.

Greenawalt, Kent. (2002). "Clear and present danger" and criminal speech. In Lee C. Bollinger and Geoffrey R. Stone (Eds.), *Eternally vigilant: Free speech in the modern era* (pp. 96–116). Chicago: The University of Chicago Press.

Habermas, Jürgen. (1973). *Theory and practice*. Boston, Beacon Press.

Habermas, Jürgen. (1979). *Communication and the evolution of society* (Thomas McCarthy, Trans.). Boston: Beacon press.

Habermas, Jürgen. (1984). *Theory of Communicative Action, Volume 1: Reason and the rationalization of society* (Thomas McCarthy, Trans.). Boston: Beacon press.

Habermas, Jürgen. (1998). *Between facts and norms: A contribution to a discourse theory of law and democracy*. Cambridge: The MIT Press.

Habermas, Jürgen. (1999). *The inclusion of the Other: Studies in political theory*. Cambridge: The MIT Press.

Hamelink, Cees J. (1997). MacBride with hindsight. In Peter Golding and Phil Harris (Eds.), *Beyond cultural imperialism: Globalization, communication and the new international order* (pp. 69–93). London: Sage.

Hamelink. Cees J. (1983). *Cultural autonomy in global communications: Planning national information policy*. New York: Longman.

Harison, Casey. (2002). Teaching the French revolution: Lessons and imagery from nineteenth and twentieth century textbooks. *History Teacher*, 35(2), 137–62.

Harley, William G. (1993). *Creative compromise: The MacBride Commission, a firsthand report and reflection on the workings of UNESCO's international commission for the study of communication problems*. New York: University Press of America.

Harms, L. S. (1977). Communication rights of mankind: Toward a multicultural worldview. In L. S. Harms, Jim Richstad and Kathleen A. Kie (Eds.), *Right to Communicate: Collected papers* (pp. 16–30). Hawaii: The University Press of Hawaii.

Harms, L. S. (1982). The Right to Communicate concept. In MacBride Commission Papers of International Communications, Collection Zimmerman, CBC/Radio-Canada. Institut International De La Communication: UNESCO.

Harms, L. S. & Richstad, Jim. (1977). Right to Communicate: Human rights, major communication issues, communication policies and planning. In L. S. Harms, Jim Richstad and Kathleen A. Kie (Eds.), *Right to Communicate: Collected papers* (pp. 94–111). Hawaii: The University Press of Hawaii.

Heath, Joseph. (2001). *Communicative action and rational choice*. London: The MIT Press.

Hobson, John Atkinson. (1902). The scientific basis of imperialism. *Political Science Quarterly, 17*(3), 460–489.

Hohfeld, Wesley Newcomb. (1919). *Fundamental legal conceptions as applied in judicial reasoning*. New Haven: Yale University Press.

Humphrey, John P. (1984). *Human rights and the United Nations: A great adventure*. New York: Transnational Publishers, Inc.

Kallen, Horace M. (1950). Human rights and the religion of John Dewey. *Ethics, 60*(3), 169–77.

Kendall, Willmoore. (1960). How to read Milton's Areopagitica. *Journal of Politics, 22*(3), 439–73.

Kramer, Matthew H. (1997). *John Locke and the origins of private property: Philosophical explorations of individualism, community, and equality*. Cambridge: Cambridge University Press.

Kramer, Matthew H. (2001). Getting rights right. In Matthew H. Kramer (Ed.), *Rights, wrongs and responsibilities* (pp. 28–95). New York: Palgrave.

Kruger, Daniel. (1955). Hobson, Lenin and Schumpeter on imperialism. *Journal of the History of Ideas, 16*(2), 252–259.

Lee, Simon. (1990). *The cost of free speech*. London. Faber and Faber.

Lerner, Daniel. (1958). *The passing of traditional society: Modernizing the Middle East*. New York: The Free Press.

Lerner, Daniel. (1980). [Review of the book *National sovereignty and international communication: A Reader*]. *Public Opinion Quarterly, 44*(1), 137–138.

Littlejohn, Stephen W. (2002). *Theories of human communication*. Australia: Wadsworth, Thomson Learning.

Locke, John. (1690a). Essay concerning human understanding. In Thomas V. Smith and Marjorie Grene (Eds.), *Philosophers speak for themselves: From Descartes to Locke* (pp. 345–354). Chicago: University of Chicago Press. [Reprinted 1940].

Locke, John. (1690b). Two treatises of government. In Thomas V. Smith and Marjorie Grene (Eds.), *From Descartes to Kant: Readings in the philosophy of the renaissance and enlightenment* (pp. 455–465). Chicago: University of Chicago Press. [Reprinted 1940].

Lyons, David. (1984). Utility and rights. In Jeremy Waldron (Ed.), *Theories of rights* (pp. 110–136). New York: Oxford University Press.

Maciak, Jill. (2001). Of news and networks: The communication of political information in the rural south-west during the French revolution. *French History, 15*(3), 273–306.

Mackie, J. L. (1984). Can there be a right-based moral theory? In Jeremy Waldron (Ed.), *Theories of rights* (pp. 168–181). New York: Oxford University Press.

Masmoudi, Mustapha. (1990). The New World Information Order. In L. John Martin and Ray Eldon Hiebert (Eds.), *Current issues in international communication* (pp. 311–320). New York: Longman.

Maxwell, Richard. (2003). *Herbert Schiller*. Lanham: Rowan & Littlefield Publishers, Inc.

Mayer, Ann-Elizabeth. (1995). *Islam and human rights: Tradition and politics.* Boulder: Westview Press.

McNitt, Andrew D. (1988). Some thoughts on the systematic measurement of the abuse of human rights. In David Louis Cingranelli (Ed.), *Human rights: Theory and measurement* (pp. 89–103). London: The Macmillan Press LTD.

McPhail, Thomas. (1981). *Electronic colonialism: The future of international broadcasting and communication.* Beverly Hills: Sage Publications.

Mill, John Stuart. (1838). Bentham. In Alan Ryan (Ed.), *John Stuart Mill and Jeremy Bentham: Utilitarianism and other essays* (pp. 132–176). London: Penguin Books. [Reprinted 1987].

Mill, John Stuart. (1859). *On liberty.* London: Penguin Classics. [Reprinted 1974].

Mill, John Stuart. (1861). Utilitarianism. In Alan Ryan (Ed.), *John Stuart Mill and Jeremy Bentham: Utilitarianism and other essays* (pp. 272–338). London: Penguin Books. [Reprinted 1987].

Milton, John. (1644). Areopagitica. In George H. Sabine (Ed.), *Areopagitica and of education.* Illinois: Harlan Davidson, Inc. [Reprinted 1951].

Montesquieu, Charles de Secondat, baron de. (1878). *The spirit of laws.* New York: Hafner Publishing. [Reprinted 1949].

Morsink, Johannes. (1999). *The Universal Declaration of Human Rights: Origins, drafting, and intent.* Philadelphia: University of Pennsylvania Press.

Mosco, Vincent. (2001). Review and criticism: Living on in the number one country, the legacy of Herbert Schiller. *Journal of Broadcasting and Electronic Media, 45*(1), 191–198.

Mowlana, Hamid. (2001). Remembering Herbert I. Schiller. *Television and New Media, 2*(1), 19–26.

Nicolson, Harold. (1960). *The age of reason: The eighteenth century*. New York: Doubleday & Company, Inc.

Nordenstreng, Kaarle & Hannikainen, Lauri. (1984). *The mass media declaration of UNESCO*. New Jersey: Ablex Publishing Corporation.

O'Rourke, K. C. (2001). *John Stuart Mill and freedom of expression: The genesis of a theory*. London: Routledge.

Palumbo, Michael. (1982). *Human rights: Meaning and history*. Malabar: Robert E. Krieger Publishing Company.

Pastecka, Jadwiga. (1982). The Right to Communicate: A socialist approach. In MacBride Commission Papers of International Communications, Collection Zimmerman, CBC/Radio-Canada. Institut International De La Communication: UNESCO.

Peters, John Durham. (1989). Democracy and American mass communication theory: Dewey, Lippmann, Lazarsfeld. *Communication, 11,* 199–220.

Peters, John Durham. (1999). *Speaking into the air: A history of the idea of communication*. Chicago: The University of Chicago Press.

Peyre, Henri. (1949). The influence of eighteenth century ideas on the French revolution. *Journal of the History of Ideas, 10*(1), 63–84.

Posner, Richard A. (2002). The speech market and the legacy of *Schenck*. In Lee C. Bollinger and Geoffrey R. Stone (Eds.), *Eternally vigilant: Free speech in the modern era* (pp. 120–151). Chicago: The University of Chicago Press.

Raz, Joseph. (1984). Right-based moralities. In Jeremy Waldron (Ed.), *Theories of rights* (pp. 182–200). New York: Oxford University Press.

Reid, John Phillip. (1986). *Constitutional history of the American revolution: The authority of rights*. Madison: The University of Wisconsin Press.

Reid, John Phillip. (1988). *The concept of liberty in the age of the American revolution*. Chicago: The University of Chicago Press.

Rendel, Margherita. (1997). *Whose human rights?* London: Trentham Books.

Renteln, Alison Dundes. (1990). *International human rights: Universalism versus relativism*. California: Sage Publications.

Richstad, Jim, Harms, L. S. & Kie, Kathleen A. (1977). The emergence of the Right to Communicate: 1970–1975. In L. S. Harms, Jim Richstad and Kathleen A. Kie (Eds.), *Right to Communicate: Collected papers* (112–136). Hawaii: The University Press of Hawaii.

Rivière, Marc Serge. (2001). Women's responses to Voltaire's writings in the eighteenth century: "A silencing of the feminine". *New Zealand Journal of French Studies*, 22(1), 5–27.

Roach, Colleen. (1997). The Western world and the NWICO: United they stand? In Peter Golding and Phil Harris (Eds.), *Beyond cultural imperialism: Globalization, communication and the new international order* (pp. 94–116). London: Sage.

Roberts, Moira. (1965). *Responsibility and practical freedom*. Cambridge: Cambridge University Press.

Salvadori, Massimo. (Ed.). (1972). *European liberalism*. New York: John Wiley & Sons, Inc.

Schiller, Herbert. (1969). *Mass communications and American empire*. Boudler: Westview Press.

Schiller, Herbert. (1976). *Communication and cultural domination*. New York: International Arts and Sciences Press.

Schiller, Herbert. (1996). *Information inequality: The deepening social crisis in America*. New York: Routledge.

Schiller, Herbert. (1998). Striving for communication dominance: A half-century review. In Daya Kishan Thussu

(Ed.), *Electronic empires: Global media and local resistance* (pp. 17–26). London: Arnold.

Schiller, Herbert. (2000). *Living in the number one country: Reflections from a critic of American empire.* New York: Seven Stories Press.

Schouls, Peter A. (1992). *Reasoned freedom: John Locke and enlightenment.* Ithaca: Cornell University Press.

Schramm, Wilbur. (1964). *Mass media and national development: The role of information in the developing countries.* Stanford: Stanford University Press and UNESCO.

Schwarzmantel, John. (1998). *The age of ideology: Political ideologies from the American revolution to postmodern times.* New York: New York University Press.

Scott, Joan Wollach. (2001). French feminists and the rights of "man": Olympe de Gouges's declarations. In Ronald Schechter (Ed.), *The French revolution* (pp. 210–235). Malden: Blackwell Publishers Ltd.

Shalin, Dmitri N. (1992). Critical theory and pragmatist challenge. *American Journal of Sociology, 98*(2), 237–79.

Shapiro, Ian. (1986). *The evolution of rights in liberal theory.* London: Cambridge University Press.

Sherman, Sandra. (1993). Printing the mind: The economics of authorship to Areopagitica. *ELH, 60*(2), 323–47.

Smolla, Rodney A. (1992). *Free speech in an open society.* New York: Alfred A. Knopf.

Stevens, John D. (1982). *Shaping the First Amendment: The development of free expression.* Beverly Hills: Sage Publications.

Stoilov, Yanaki B. (2001). Are human rights universal? In Burton M. Leiser and Tom D. Campbell (Eds.), *Human rights in philosophy and practice* (pp. 87–104). Aldershot, England: Dartmouth, Ashgate Publishing Limited.

Thussu, Daya Kishan. (2000). *International communication: Continuity and change.* London: Arnold.

Tomlinson, John. (1991). *Cultural imperialism: A critical introduction*. London: Printer Publishers.

Traber, Michael & Nordenstreng, Kaarle. (Eds.). (1992). *Few voices, many worlds: Towards a media reform movement*. London: World Association for Christian Communication.

Waldron, Jeremy. (Ed.). (1984). *Theories of rights*. New York: Oxford University Press.

Wallerstein, Immanuel. (1974). The rise and future demise of the world capitalist system: Concepts for comparative analysis. *Comparative Studies in Society and History*, 16(4), 387–415

Wallerstein, Immanuel. (1976). Semi-peripheral countries and the contemporary world crisis. *Theory and Society*, 3, 461–484.

Wasserstrom, Richard. (1979). Right, human rights, and racial discrimination. In David Lyons (Ed.), *Rights* (pp. 46–57). Belmont: Wadsworth Publishing Company, Inc.

Williams, David (Ed.). (1994). *Voltaire political writings*. Cambridge: Cambridge University Press.

Author Index

A
Ali, Shaheen Sardar, 175
Allen, R. E., 175
Amin, Samir, 49, 175
Anderson, Debra J., 175
Antonio, Robert J., 175

B
Baehr, Peter R., 175
Baker, Keith Michael, 175
Barron, Jerome A., 175
Bentham, Jeremy, 9, 84, 104–8, 175, 177, 183
Bernier, Olivier, 176
Bollinger, Lee C., 180, 184
Bordas, Eric, 176
Boylan, James, 176
Bradley, A. W., 176
Breckheimer, P. J., 176
Brems, Eva, 176

C
Campbell, Tom D., 179, 186
Chartier, Roger, 176
Chase, Bob, 115, 176
Cingranelli, David Louis, 183
Cocca, Aldo Armando, 68, 176
Creppell, Ingrid, 177
Cutler, Fred, 177

D
d'Arcy, Jean, 32–33, 44, 47, 60, 63, 64, 171, 172
Dakroury, Aliaa, 177, 178

Darnton, Robert, 178
Dennis, Everette E., 178
Dewey, John, 9, 118–24, 178, 181
Dienes, Thomas C., 175
Donnelly, Jack, 92, 178
Dorfman, Ariel, 178
Douzinas, Costas, 17, 178
Dunne, Tim, 178

F
Fairchilds, Cissie, 24, 45, 178
Feinberg, Joel, 178
Fireman, Peter, 178
Fisher, Desmond, 179
Fisher, John, 179
Freeman, Michael, 179
Froman, Creel, 179
Furet, François, 17, 179

G
Garnham, Nicholas, 179
Geuss, Raymond, 81, 179
Gewirth, Alan, 179
Giddens, Anthony, 179
Gill, Emily R., 179
Glendon, Mary Ann, 179
Golding, Peter, 180, 185
Gray, John, 180
Greenawalt, Kent, 180
Grene, Marjorie, 182

H
Haakonssen, Knud, 180
Habermas, Jürgen, 9, 18, 105, 118, 124–36, 179, 180
Hamelink, Cees J., 180
Hannikainen, Lauri, 184
Harison, Casey, 45, 180

Harley, William G., 180
Harms, L. S., 35, 177, 181, 185
Harris, Phil, 180, 185
Heath, Joseph, 181
Hiebert, Ray Eldon, 183
Hobson, John Atkinson, 152, 181
Hohfeld, Wesley Newcomb, 70, 181
Humphrey, John P., 181

K
Kallen, Horace M., 181
Kendall, Willmoore, 181
Kie, Kathleen A., 177, 181, 185
Kramer, Matthew H., 181, 182
Kruger, Daniel, 151, 182

L
Lee, Simon, 80, 182
Leiser, Burton M., 186
Lerner, Daniel, 39, 41, 150, 182
Littlejohn, Stephen W., 182
Locke, John, 9, 84, 91–96, 115, 133, 176, 180, 181, 182, 186, 191
Lyons, David, 178, 182, 187

M
Maciak, Jill, 19, 182
Mackie, J. L., 182
Major, Robert L., 175
Martin, L. John, 183
Masmoudi, Mustapha, 183
Mattelart, Armand, 156, 178
Maxwell, Richard, 137, 183
Mayer, Ann-Elizabeth, 183
McCarthy, Thomas, 180
McNitt, Andrew D., 69, 183
McPhail, Thomas, 183
Merrill, John C., 178

Mill, John Stuart, 9, 84, 105–6, 107–14, 175, 180, 183, 184
Milton, John, 9, 84–91, 183
Montesquieu, Charles de Secondat, baron de, 9, 96–99, 183
Morsink, Johannes, 183
Mosco, Vincent, 137, 184
Mowlana, Hamid, 143, 184

N
Nicolson, Harold, 184
Nordenstreng, Kaarle, 184, 187

O
O'Rourke, K. C., 111, 184

P
Palumbo, Michael, 184
Panagiotou, Spiro, 175
Pastecka, Jadwiga, 166–67, 184
Peters, John Durham, 184
Peyre, Henri, 184
Posner, Richard A., 184

R
Raz, Joseph, 77, 184
Reid, John Phillip, 185
Rendel, Margherita, 185
Renteln, Alison Dundes, 69, 185
Richstad, Jim, 177, 181, 185
Rivière, Marc Serge, 185
Roach, Colleen, 185
Roberts, Moira, 185
Ryan, Alan, 175, 183

S
Sabine, George H., 183
Salvadori, Massimo, 185
Schechter, Ronald, 175, 176, 178, 186

Schiller, Herbert, 9, 10, 43, 118, 136–48, 164, 183, 184, 185–86
Schouls, Peter A., 186
Schramm, Wilbur, 39, 41, 186
Schwarzmantel, John, 186
Scott, Joan Wollach, 186
Shalin, Dmitri N., 186
Shapiro, Ian, 186
Sherman, Sandra, 186
Skinner, Quentin, 179
Smith, Thomas V., 182
Smolla, Rodney A., 186
Stevens, John D., 186
Stoilov, Yanaki B., 186
Stone, Geoffrey R., 180, 184

T
Thussu, Daya Kishan, 185–86, 186
Tomlinson, John, 187
Traber, Michael, 187

W
Waldron, Jeremy, 179, 182, 187
Wallerstein, Immanuel, 139, 145, 151, 187
Wasserstrom, Richard, 187
Wheeler, Nicholas, 178
Williams, David, 187

Subject Index

A
ABC Dialogues: Seventeen, The, 99–100
Absolute free speech, 55–56
Absolute freedom of speech, 9, 99–104, 126
Absolute right to communicate, 54–61, 79, 98, 99–104, 114, 120, 129, 162, 171
Age of Reason, 84, 184
American pragmatism, 125, 149
American Revolution, 17–18, 19, 20, 45
Ancien régime, 17, 18
Anti-propaganda, 54
Anti-war, 62, 139
Areopagitica, 85–89
Article (19), 26, 29–31, 32, 53, 60–61, 64
Authorship, 84, 90, 100, 161

B
Bad book, 19, 88–90, 113, 161
Basic human rights. *See* Human rights
Bentham, Jeremy, 9, 84, 104–8
Bible, 92
Bill of Rights
    American, 13, 14, 15–17
    English, 17
Book-burning principle, 88
Bosnia, 163
British colony, 17
British sovereignty, 17
Brotherhood of man, 4, 11

C
Cable, 64
Canada, 34, 47, 58, 59, 80, 154

Canadian Broadcasting Act (1968), 33–34
Cassin, Réné, 46, 61
Censorship, 2, 3–6, 46, 65, 84–90, 100–101, 113, 161
Chicago School, 118
Christianity, 5–6, 56, 84, 92
Church of England Group, 56
Cicero, Marcus Tillius, 4, 11
Class, 25, 123, 138, 145
Clear and present danger, 61–63
Collective will, 53
Collectiveness, 68, 77
Collectivity, 28, 68
Colonizing, 133–34
Comédie Francaise, 23
Commonwealth, 83, 93
Communication
    corporations, 64
    history of, 13–44, 19
    human rights and, 1–10, 36–37, 58, 61, 163
    industry, 63
    institutions, 169
    inter-personal, 27, 48, 171
    language and, 159–60
    media, 8, 53, 63–64, 86–87, 100–101, 141–43, 148, 165
    philosophical foundation of, 83–114
    right to communicate and, 51–79, 159–73
    technologies, 63–64, 151, 164
    theorization of, 117–49
Communicative model, 133
Community, 119–20, 125, 130
Conglomerate media ownership, 52, 63–65
Congress, 13, 15, 16, 62
Conscience, 77–78, 85, 88–89, 92
Conscious communication, 171
Constitutional laws, 16, 29
Constitutional regulations, 16
Convergence, 64

Copyright, 4, 61
Criminals, 6, 127, 129, 132
Crisis, 45
Culture, 42–44, 152–157
　　media and, 39–41
　　right to communicate and, 10, 118, 136–49

D
dArcy, Jean, 32–33, 44, 47, 60, 63, 64, 171, 172
Decision making, 110
Déclaration des Droits de l'Homme et du Citoyen, 17–25
Déclaration des Droits de la Femme et de la Citoyenne, 22
Declaration of Independence, 15, 21, 28, 122, 162–63
Declaration of the Rights of the Man and of the Citizen, 21
Decolonization, 37, 134, 140
Defamation, 56
Democracy, 17–18, 45–46, 97–98, 119–24, 173
Democratic society, 34, 80, 165
Department of Free Flow of Information and
　　Development, 165
Déscartes, René, 91
Developed countries, 31, 40, 128, 140
Developing countries, 31, 38–43, 49, 127–29, 142–45, 150, 152
Dewey, John, 9, 118–24, 125
Dialogue, 10, 43, 118–124, 133
Disability, 71, 73
Distorted communication, 127
Diversity, 64, 70, 99
Diversity of opinion, 64
Divine, 4, 55, 69, 77
Duty, 11, 53, 71–79, 88, 104, 122, 134, 136, 170–71

E
Economic prosperity, 62
Education, 73, 76
Educational rights, 163
English men, 89

Enlightenment
    ideology, 18
    philosophers, 94, 132
    principles, 18, 25
Equal, 6, 21, 24, 28, 54, 66, 77, 93, 135, 162–63
Equality, 3, 6, 20, 77, 93, 97, 99, 104, 139–40, 142
Equity, 21, 65
Espionage Act, 62
Esprit des Lois, 96–97
Essay Concerning Human Understanding (Locke), 94, 96
Essay on the Laws of Nature (Locke), 94–95
Ethics, 2–3, 65, 124, 164, 169, 172, 173
European, 18, 33, 154
Evil, 88–90, 110, 113

F
Faculty of reason, 87
False, 88, 89, 168, 169
Fascism, 29, 53–55
Fatwa, 56
Feminist, 22, 24, 58, 104
First amendment, 59, 62–63, 162–63
Flow of information, 2, 8, 37–41, 128, 145, 147
France, 14, 18, 19–22
Fraternity, 20
Free, 12, 15, 16, 21–23, 25–26, 28, 77, 93, 115
Free flow of information, 37–38, 106, 136, 165
Free speech, 1–6, 9, 13, 15, 17, 19–27, 29–30, 34, 36, 61–65, 80, 90. *See also* Speech
Freedom
    from fear, 27
    from want, 27
    of authorship, 84, 90
    of clothes, 24–25
    of communication, 85
    of conscience, 85
    of expression, 9, 14, 24–25, 32–33, 55, 104–8, 127–28

of inquiry, 117, 120, 149
of opinion, 14, 20, 36, 112, 127–28
of speech, 1–6, 9, 13, 15, 17, 19–27, 29–30, 34, 36, 61–65, 80, 90
of the press, 15–16, 20, 84, 105
of thought, 4, 19, 87, 93, 95, 109–10, 161
of worship, 27
to disseminate and access information and ideas, 87
French Convention of the Freedom of Dress, 24–25
French Declaration, 8, 20, 21, 23–26, 28, 93
French National Assembly, 20
French National Convention, 22–23
French Revolution, 17–26, 45, 160, 161
Frontier, 86
Fundamental freedoms, 26, 134, 135
Fundamental human rights, 26, 55, 67

G
Gay and lesbian rights, 66
General Assembly of the United Nations, 26, 36
Generations, 53, 66
Germany, 27, 35, 41, 120, 137, 138, 150
God, 6, 56, 77–78, 86, 96
Good book, 88
Government, 105, 123, 145, 147
Government policies
Greatest happiness, 9, 106, 107, 108–14
Greek, 2–5

H
Habeas Corpus Act (England 1679), 66
Habermas, Jürgen, 9, 18, 105, 118, 124–36
Hate speech, 9, 52, 69–70, 80, 125–30, 162, 172
	vs. free speech, 55–57
Health care, 78
History of communication, 19
History of human rights, 84

Hitler, Adolph, 29
Hohfeld, Wesley, 51
Horizontal flow of information, 60–61
Horizontal integration, 64
House of Commons, 59
Human dignity, 55, 59, 84
Human liberty, 94, 97
Human rights, 1–10
    basic, 8–10
    fundamental, 26, 55, 67
    history of, 84
    international recognition of, 26
    violations of, 27, 29
Human Rights Commission, 29, 46
Human rights violations, 27, 29
Humanism, 77
Humanity, 24, 57, 124, 160–61

I
Ideal speech situation, 125, 132, 164
Immoral, 88, 113
Immunity, 71, 73, 111–12
Immunity-disability, 73
Individual freedom, 103, 160
Individual liberty, 95
Individual rights, 18, 54
Individuality, 24, 28, 53, 68, 109, 121
Inherent rights, 15
Inhumanity, 102
Instant World report, 34
Interest theory, 74
Inter-group communication, 132, 171
International community, 37, 45, 54
International Covenant on Civil and Political Rights (1966), 14, 32, 36, 60, 67, 160
International Covenant on Economic, Social and Cultural Rights, 32, 160
International Institute of Communications (IIC), 35, 47

International recognition of human rights, 26
International resolutions, 35
International treatises, 67
Internet, 4, 57–59, 140, 148
Inter-personal communication, 27, 171
Intolerance, 55–56, 57, 92, 102
Intuition, 69
Islam, 5, 6, 11

J
Jefferson, Thomas, 21
Jesus, 5
Journalism, 168–69
Journalists' right to communicate, 37, 52, 163, 169
Judaism, 5
Justice, 2–6, 18, 28, 162

K
Kant, Immanuel, 104
Knowledge, 11, 34, 88–90, 94–95, 133

L
Lafayette, 20–21
Language, 5, 7, 10, 18, 26–28, 30, 96, 115, 119, 127, 132, 133, 149, 162
Law, 4, 16, 26, 56–57, 60–61, 78, 99, 101, 129, 133
Leadership, 107
Legal
    community, 132
    institutions, 14
    judgment, 16
    rights, 16, 70, 74, 81, 107
Legislative, 36, 97
Liability, 71, 73
Libelles, 20
Liberalism, 16, 92, 122, 133
Liberty, 15–17, 20–26, 72–73, 84–85, 94–104, 109–12

Licensor, 85–87
Literate, 84, 87, 88, 89
Living intellect, 86
Locke, John, 9, 84, 91–96, 133
    Essay Concerning Human Understanding, 94, 96
    Essay on the Laws of Nature, 94–95

M

MacBride Commission, 8, 10, 41–44, 61, 68, 137, 166
MacBride Commission Report, 61, 166
MacBride, Seán, 42
Magna Carta, 6, 7, 17, 31
Manipulating, 120, 130
Mass media, 27, 36, 39, 40, 54, 132, 163, 173
Mastery, 88, 91, 94, 96
Media, 1–2, 8–9, 19, 39–41
    ownership and control, 9, 52, 63–65
    technologies, 31
    UNESCO *Media Declaration*, 8, 14, 31, 34–37, 67
Mental freedom, 94
Mill, John Stuart, 9, 84, 105–114
Milton, John, 9, 84–91
Minority, 42, 110
Modern liberal, 92
Modern media technologies, 31
Monarchies, 98
Monopolies, 40, 63, 145
Montesquieu, Baron de, 9, 96–99
Moral boundaries, 99
Moral norms, 132
Moral rights, 70
Moral rules, 3, 99
Morality, 21, 65, 70, 75, 77, 89, 104, 108–9, 132–33, 162
    Islamic, 6
    religion and, 92
    sexual, 59
    universal, 68–69, 132–33
Muslims, 52, 55, 56

N

National, 23, 43–44, 55, 60, 123, 134, 143, 160, 163, 173
National territory, 123
Natural Law, 4, 18, 53, 69, 92
Natural rights, 4, 21, 25, 69, 77, 92, 106, 107
Nazis, 27, 29–30, 46, 52, 53
New World Information and Communication Order (NWICO) debate, 127–28
New world information order, 42
News agencies, 42, 169
Newspapers, 19, 27, 30, 64, 105, 163, 172
Non-aligned movement, 35, 38
No-right, 71, 72
Normative standards, 99
Normative validity, 132
Norms, 40, 67, 122, 125–26, 128–29, 131–34, 149, 164, 173
North America, 58, 137

O

Obligation, 36, 68, 71–72, 77, 107, 126–27, 130, 169
Of the Conduct of the Understanding (Locke), 93
Old Testament, 5
Olympe de Gouges,
On Liberty (Mill), 109–11
Opinion, 1–37, 55, 57, 62, 64, 90, 92–99, 104–8, 109–12
Oppression, 3, 21, 92, 161
Oral communication, 19

P

Pamphlets, 19, 20
Peace, 16, 28, 55, 62, 66, 123
Personal communication, 121
Personal happiness, 62
Personal liberty, 101
Personal property, 109
Philosophical liberty, 96, 97

Philosophers
    Bentham, Jeremy, 104–8
    Dewey, John, 118–24
    Habermas, Jurgen, 124–36
    Locke, John, 91–96
    Mill, John Stuart, 108–14
    Milton, John, 84–91
    Montesquieu, Baron de, 96–99
    Schiller, Herbert, 136–49
Philosophy, 3–4, 15, 160–61, 163
    natural rights and, 25
Physical control, 87
Plato, 5, 92
Policy, 5, 20, 27, 43, 105, 109, 111, 169
Political activist, 23
Political changes, 35
Political independence, 17
Political liberty, 25, 96, 97
Political organization, 123
Political power, 92–93, 100, 105
Political public opinion, 19
Political reform, 18
Political stability, 1, 62
Political system, 99, 162
Pornography, 9, 52, 57, 65, 112–13, 125, 129, 130
Positive law, 69, 77, 96, 97
Post-publication, 90
Power relations, 35, 73, 138, 141, 143, 164
Power-liability, 72
Pre-publication censorship, 84, 86
Press, the, 32, 46–47, 90, 105, 132,
    freedom of, 15–16, 20–21, 25, 29, 84–86, 101, 105, 161–62
Printing, 30, 40, 83, 86, 100
Privacy, 9, 170
    invasion of, 59–63
Private property, 92
Privilege, 25, 34, 51, 71, 72, 77

"Privilege-No right" (relationship), 72
Progress, 55, 91, 120
Propaganda, 4, 9, 27, 29, 47, 52–55, 69, 120–121, 164
Property, 7, 15, 21, 22, 29, 92, 95, 109
Prophet, 6, 52, 55–56
Protection, 17, 27–28, 75, 110–11, 122
    First Amendment and, 59
    law and, 57, 45, 107, 129–30
    liberty and, 99
    media and, 37
    Right to Communicate and, 133
Protestantism, 125
Protests, 27
Public good, 77
Public opinion, 9, 19, 104–06
Public opinion tribunal, 105
Public policies, 27
Public speaking, 88
Public sphere, 3, 4, 7, 19, 23, 105, 107
Pursuit of happiness, 15

Q
Qur'an, 6

R
Race, 26, 66, 91, 110, 123
Racist political message, 52
Ratification of international treaties, 69
Rational communicative consensus, 133
Rational discourses, 133
Rationality, 91, 94, 96, 121, 130–31
Reason, 18, 84, 86–87, 91, 96, 121, 147
Reciprocal communication, 128
Reform, 18, 19, 20
Regional, 67, 125, 134, 163
Regulations, 1, 16, 67, 69, 99, 125, 138, 169

Religion, 5, 92, 100–103, 133
    freedom of, 13, 15–16, 26, 57, 123
    rights and, 66, 68–69
Religious beliefs, 56, 69
Religious intolerance, 92
Republicanism, 133
Republic, The, (Plato), 3
Responsibility, 10, 73–75, 77, 79, 130, 132, 171
Rhetoric, 3, 6, 88
Right, 2, 20–26, 27–28, 29–31, 32–34, 35
    defined, 65–79
    of access to information, 106
    to free speech, 52, 58, 110, 132
    to freedom of opinion, 14, 29, 36
    to marry, 66
    to "not" communicate, 59–63
    to privacy, 59–61
    of man, 13, 21–24, 31
Right to communicate, 5, 8–10, 13–16; 34, 159–73
    basic rights and, 170–73
    language and, 159–60
    perspectives on, 166–70
    practice debate, 162–66
    realization phase, 160–62
Roman, 4, 5
Roosevelt, Franklin, 27
Royal commission, 58
Rule of law, 133
Rwanda, 163

S
Sacred, 20, 21, 57, 86
Safety, 15, 74
Satanic Verses, The, 52, 55, 56
Satirical writings, 98
Schiller, Herbert, 9, 10, 43, 118, 136–49, 164
Scientific method, 117, 120, 149

Second Treatise on Government (Locke), 92
Security, 21, 60, 66
Sex, 23, 24, 25, 26, 59
Slavery of the mind, 100
Slippery slope, 65
Social change, 17, 39, 40
Social class, 25
Social system, 97, 99, 122
Social thinking, 120, 167
Social values, 128, 148, 172
Socialist, 31, 166, 167
Socrates, 3
Sovereignty, 17, 18, 92, 133
Speech
    Bentham, Jeremy and, 104–7
    freedom of, 1–6, 9, 13, 15, 17, 19–27, 29–30, 34, 36, 61–65, 80, 90
    hate vs. free, 9, 52, 55–57, 69–70, 80
    internet and, 57–59
    invasion of privacy and, 59–63
    Milton, John, and 90, 92, 93–96
    Montesquieu, Baron de and, 98–99
    pornography and, 57–59
    right to communication and, 57–59
    Voltaire and, 99–104
State, 3, 31, 45, 59, 60, 71, 78, 94, 96, 120, 134
Supreme Court, 57, 58

T
Table of jural correlatives, 71
Telecommission Studies, 33–34, 47
Telecommunication, 34, 47, 63, 64
Television stations, 64
Terrorism, 60, 170
Theatres, 27
Theory of communicative action, 124, 125

Third World, 31, 38–43, 49, 50, 127–28, 143–49. *See also* Developing countries
Tolerance, 55, 92, 102, 162
Toleration, 100, 102, 117, 120, 149
Toleration principle in communication, 102
Totalitarianism and propaganda, 52–55
Totalitarian regime, 27, 29, 53, 65, 120
Traditions, 5, 44, 53, 67, 128, 134, 149
Traité sur la Tolérance, 102
True Christian, 88, 102, 113
Truth, 3–4, 11, 23, 84, 89, 101, 109, 129, 169
    political, 122–23

U
Unalienable right, 15
Uncensored, 89
Undistorted communication, 10, 124, 125, 126, 127, 131
United Nations Educational, Scientific and Cultural Organization (UNESCO), 32, 35, 37, 38, 41, 42, 44, 54, 147, 165
    Media Declaration, 8, 14, 31, 34–37, 67
    meeting of Experts on Mass Communication and Society, 35
Uni-dimensional right to communicate (Milton), 9, 84–91
United Nations, 8, 26, 30, 36, 41, 42, 55, 60, 61, 134, 135, 147
United Nations Charter (1945), 26
Universal
    access, 64
    human right, 56
    morality, 68
    right, 57, 58, 132
    validity claims, 125, 126
Universal Declaration of Human Rights, 4, 14, 26–33, 36–37, 46, 52–55, 58–67, 93–94, 133–35
    language and, 26–28
    right to communicate since, 31–34
Universal Islamic Declaration of Human Rights, 6, 11

U.S. Supreme Court, 57, 58
USSR, 29
Utilitarianism, 70, 108
Utility, 77, 83, 108, 109, 112, 113
Utopian ideal, 18, 164

V
Validity claims, 125–32, 164, 169, 172
Values, 61, 67–70, 132
    androcentric, 104
    capitalistic, 146–47
    Christian, 161–62
    conflicting, 55–56, 120–22
    MacBride Commission Report and, 166–67
    Protestant, 125
    societal, 120–23, 126, 128–31, 145, 148–49, 164, 172
Van Gogh, 27
Verbal expression, 57
Vienna Declaration (1993), 134
Violation
    of Article (19), 64
    of expression, 46
    of law, 78
    of Right to Communicate, 84, 112–14, 148–49, 164
    of rights, 7, 26–28, 45–46, 69–71, 87, 92, 100–101, 149, 163
Violence, 57, 92, 102
Violence against women, 58
Violence in society, 57
Virginia Declaration (1776), 15, 28
Voltaire, 19, 84, 91, 113, 114, 118, 162
    Absolute freedom of speech and, 9, 99–104
    Candide (Dr. Pangloss), 37, 48
    Lettres sur les Anglais, 91–92

W
Weak communication, 132
Western cultural, 27, 144

Will Theory, 74
Wisdom, 89
Women's rights, 22, 23
World War I (WWI), 62
World War II (WWII), 26, 31, 45